THE WOMAN IN THE MIRROR

A Survivor's Journey into the Authentic Self

EVELYN MEJIL

ARCHWAY
PUBLISHING

This book is a work of non-fiction. Unless otherwise noted, the author and the publisher make no explicit guarantees as to the accuracy of the information contained in this book and in some cases, names of people and places have been altered to protect their privacy.

Archway Publishing books may be ordered through booksellers or by contacting:

Archway Publishing
1663 Liberty Drive
Bloomington, IN 47403
www.archwaypublishing.com
1 (888) 242-5904

Because of the dynamic nature of the Internet, any web addresses or links contained in this book may have changed since publication and may no longer be valid. The views expressed in this work are solely those of the author and do not necessarily reflect the views of the publisher, and the publisher hereby disclaims any responsibility for them.

Any people depicted in stock imagery provided by Getty Images are models, and such images are being used for illustrative purposes only. Certain stock imagery © Getty Images.

ISBN: 978-1-4808-6710-9 (sc)
ISBN: 978-1-4808-6709-3 (e)

Library of Congress Control Number: 2018909643

Print information available on the last page.

Archway Publishing rev. date: 10/17/2018

You can run from the burning passion
ignited in your heart because of fear:
fear of what people will say;
fear of the way in which people will judge you;
fear of the way in which people will criticize you;
fear of those who will try to stop you;
fear of those who will try to quench your fire;
fear of those who will leave you;
fear of those you will leave;
fear of being misunderstood;
fear of your pain;
fear of your past;
fear of wanting more;
fear of your dreams;
fear of your potential;
fear of fear.
Or you can become that which you fear the most:
that which burns in you like fire;
that which your heart desires;
that which is truth;
that which is power;
that which is you,
the authentic self.

To my brother Danny.
You will always have life in my heart.
I love you, always and forever.

Contents

Acknowledgments

It is my great privilege to honor those who have honored me by loving me unconditionally and seeing what I couldn't see in me, until I did.

First, to my mother, thank you for choosing to give me life and being the instrument to bring forth my essence into this world. My greatest lesson in love is you. I will honor you with my life, and I will love you through all my existence. To my dad, you chose to fill someone else's shoes, but to me, they have always and will always belong to you. I love you deeply. To my brothers: Jose and Carlos. Jose, thank you for being a role model of strength, integrity, and faith. I love you for everything that you are and for everything you inspire me to be. My baby brother, Carlos, you had to be the last, because everything that is good in all of us was perfected in you. Thank you for being my compass and always guiding me to the heart of me without judgment and with unconditional love. I love you beyond words and beyond this lifetime. To my nieces and nephew, Kryzzia, Kiara, Keishla, Amber, Yamilex, and Ashley, the queens of my heart, and Justin, my sweet prince, you are my greatest love of all. To my great grandmother and grandmother, our matriarchs— thank you for being the strength, the wisdom, and the force of life that still lives in me, for me and through me. I honor you. Thank you for filling my spirit.

To my two greatest inspirations—my mentors and my angels— Liz Hevia and Donald Bey. You nursed my heart and healed my soul. You gave me the gift of life, I hope to forever honor you with my life.

Thank you for being my beacon of light, hope and strength. Because of you, I am. To my spiritual parents and guide, Dr. Iko Ibanga, Esther Ibanga, Michael Howell and the legendary Gloria Gaynor, thank you for lighting up my path and nurturing my soul with your wisdom and love.

I want to make a special mention and thank those special people in my heart and at the heart of bringing this book to life. Every phase of this book had each of you as its guardian angel. You have been my light in navigating the darkest corners of my past, the balm for my pain, and you held on to me, so I could finally let go. You were my support and the faith that kept me going. You gave me a new dream and a new hope when you took this journey with me. I don't have the words to thank you for nurturing my spirit and loving me unconditionally. The core of my being and my anchors, Ruthy, Damaris, Nydia, Donald, and Orlando, I love you to infinity and beyond. Thank you.

To my women tribe in Malaysia and Thailand. Madeleine, thank you for allowing yourself to be the conduit of the most powerful journey of all, facing my pain and being with my pain. You helped me to stop running and fearing my pain. You held a space for me, and I was finally able to be in my truth. Mariza, thank you for showing me the power of love and being love when I needed it the most. Natasya, thank you for teaching me about self-worth and the strength in knowing my value. Masuri, thank you for being all that is grace; your essence is forever so powerfully present. Farah, thank you for being my mirror and not allowing me to run from myself. Shaney, thank you; you were the instrument that brought it all to life for me. Thank you for believing with me and for me. To you, my sweet friend, I say our end was only the beginning, and, Pam, thank you for being my rock and being my home until I finally found my home in the heart of me. I love you all dearly.

Lastly, my band of sisters, my beautiful tribe of women, and my heroines, you are part of my life's journey. Each of you entered my life as family or during life-defining moments that transformed our friendships into a sisterhood and created bonds that will last a lifetime. Because of your strength, wisdom, beauty, talent, and power, I am a better woman. I am deeply grateful for each of you and for you being part of my journey. Thank you for inspiring me, believing in me, and supporting me, but above all, thank you for being you. I honor you: Mildred, Maria Cristina, Celina, Maria, Luisa, Zenaida, Jessica, Cathy, Beverly, Mayaly, Alexa, Judy, Carolina, Paula, Ruthy, Damaris, Eileen, Stephanie, Ranice, Charisse, Marilyn, Marisol, Nydia, Neuza, Jackie, Haydee, Jeannine, Fiordaliza, Dihanna, Denise, Lee, Cindy, Anthea, Caroline, Pam, Martha, Mica, Faith, Shraddha, Evelyn, Betsy, Jeannette, Sabrina, Brittany, Madeline, Janetza, Tatiana, and my dear Melissa. To my superheroes, Charles, Brian, Orlando, Alex, Juan A., Juan, Raniel and Ariso, you lift up the women in your lives like queens. You hold a special place in my heart my brothers. Thank you for lifting me up and never allowing me to stop believing. To my special angels, Leilani, Anthony, Melany, Alejandro and Javier, you're my fireflies, lighting up my heart.

Thank you to the people who inspired me along the way. Above all, thankful to God for the gift of life, light, and everlasting love. My spirit rejoices, my cup runneth over, and my heart is full. Lastly, thank you to my beautiful surprise, love. Your timing was perfect my sweet love. I give you, my authentic self. Always and forever.

THE WOMAN IN THE MIRROR

I once stood before a young woman who was on the verge of ending her life. I stared into her eyes and watched as she drowned herself in tears of pain, shame, and hurt. She looked directly into my eyes, and I felt the weight of her helplessness and confusion. She cried out in desperation, asking for an explanation why her life had been filled with so much anguish. She thought about the nightmares that were her constant nocturnal companions and did not allow her to forget. She remembered waking up in rumpled, sweaty sheets, feeling the cold, gripping fingers of her memories as they violated her again and again; the cold tentacles of terror that came over her each time she relived the agony of being dishonored, every disgusting touch and every brutal strike. Although she held up her hands to cover her ears, she could still hear every dreadful word ever spoken to her, the voices echoing in the emptiness of her hollow heart. Regardless of how many tears she shed, they couldn't wash away the suffering of her soul. The weight of abuse became unbearable and too much for her to carry alone.

The woman I saw was me, peering into a mirror.

A Survivor's Journey into the Authentic Self

Our lives are the sum of many parts, and it is our hope that the sum forms a harmonious whole. Our balance is suspended in the synergy between two complex natures: our relationships with the world and with the self. The two are the sum of our existence. We all share the same experiences; however, the uniqueness of our individual experiences stems from the uniqueness that emanates from our inner being. For this reason, we must know if what we are emanating is our authentic self or one that lies in its shadow, the false self.

The false self is an identity we create that suppresses our authenticity when it is oppressed by pain, unworthiness, and shame. We create the false self when we allow painful circumstances to define us. The greater the pain, the greater the distance we create from our purest nature. Consequently, an imminent disconnect is inevitable, and we neglect our most substantial source of life: the authenticity that comes from within, our spirit nature.

Pain has many of us living as though our essence has no escape from the world in which our experiences have been formed. Rather than allowing our relationship with our inner being to shape our experiences, we have allowed our experiences to define our inner being.

Spirit is the driving force of life, the architect of our authentic self, and the author of our fate. It is that essence that makes the difference between how we live our lives today and our unwritten destiny. It knows no limits. It is the freedom that breaks all bonds to traumatic past events and crippling relationships. It has the strength that we lack, the vision we have lost, and the determination that has faltered in the face of our disillusionment. It carries the hope we need, and it is the faith that allows us to embark on a journey back to our true selves. All in all, it is the lost identity that seeks to permeate our essence to allow the truest expression of the self.

Spirit is the source of all truth—the truth we seek outside ourselves but cannot find because we fail to realize it lies within. Spirit cannot be defined by human affliction or characterized by the ailments of our experiences. It is greater than all sources of pain, and its nature prevails through our greatest sorrow. However, the traits of pain in our human experiences begin to mold us and somehow to define us. Yet we are not defined by the experiences that occur in the natural realm. Our spirit defines who we truly are, reveals our purpose, and creates balance. Spirit is perfect, whole, and complete. It embodies our true essence, so our being can express it.

Spirit transmutes into every living experience, but when the sum of our experiences is outweighed by the grief and toxic relationships that have ravaged our lives, our spirit becomes buried in the depths of emotions, feelings, thoughts, and ideas that originate in our false self. Our veiled truth allows unhappiness to begin to steer our lives into what feels like an unending abyss in the vast of the unknown and with no horizon in sight.

In the absence of our authentic self, our destiny becomes entangled in our false self and life seems to dismantle itself at every step. However, we do not create our authentic self, and therefore, it can never be destroyed. Our authentic self is our being, the spirit of life that flows through us and in us in each moment. We simply have become preoccupied with the illusion that the present is filled with the past and that somehow it dictates our present, so we also begin to worry about the future. Nonetheless, the gift of you lies simply in all present moments. You are the gift for which you have been waiting.

The desire to fill our voids is simply our heart-mind communicating our authenticity, willing its most powerful expression. But when our heart's desire is to fulfill our purpose and live out our destiny, all things conspire to reveal our truth.

On an inconspicuous and unexpected day, a thought takes center stage in our minds, we begin to question and reflect on the purpose of our lives, and a desire awakens that demands an answer. We are unaware of what prompts this sudden shift in consciousness, except that we have reached a crossroads. The process leads us to ponder the circumstances that depict our life as we know it, creating an unpredictable yearning to discover who we are and the true meaning of our existence.

Our core becomes overwhelmed with questions such as, what is my destiny? Can I ever truly be happy? What is happiness? Is my life a façade? These were some of my ruminations, all of which led to the ultimate questions of who am I and what is my purpose? The initial answers lead to an unsettling truth that ultimately becomes an incomprehensible but vigorous source of strength in our quest for our true selves.

I did not know who I was immediately, but I knew immediately who I was not. I was neither my past nor my titles or positions.

In our quest for answers, we experience many moments of enlightenment that continue to fuel our inner strength. These moments assume a rare life of their own and direct us to a turning point that takes us on an unforgettable journey.

The journey on which we embark sometimes brings us to a halt and forces us to reflect on the circumstances and relationships of our lives. The dynamics of our relationships will become clear, and our circumstances will begin to lose meaning so that they can have real meaning. We will seek to understand the role we play in our relationships and the events that define us, and in these circumstances, we will begin to rewrite our story. We become engrossed in the pursuit and aware of that which has impoverished our spirit. Finally, a mirror is unveiled, the lies are dismantled, the process reveals the answers we seek, we are awakened, and we continue to journey deeper within.

When the process of life leads us back to ourselves, the world as we know it begins to lose its reason for being. Nothing makes sense. It is as if the people and situations in our lives become a fictional story, and a nagging, hollow feeling in our heart that we cannot ignore assures us this is not our story. What our minds could not conceive suddenly becomes the conundrum of our lives. Thoughts arise that shift the foundations of our being, but we don't know why. All we can fathom is that our world has sunk in a deep sea of questions that separate our past from our destiny.

Oftentimes throughout our journey, we will find ourselves in a foreign place. Our thoughts become unfamiliar. The way we view that world is novel. Yet there is an unreasonable belief that where our journey is leading us is exactly where we need to be. Familiarity begins to feel uncomfortable; something inside us rejects it. It no longer feels safe and secure but turns dull and lifeless instead. The things that have kept us stagnant begin to surface. And amid all, our old story begins to dig its claws into every new thought and floods our emotions. Uncertainty consumes us because of the disenchantment we feel that we no longer fit in the world we once knew.

So many questions will bombard our minds all at once that for a time silence will feel merciless. The uncertainty of why the things in our lives have lost their significance will leave us wondering if we truly have strayed from our course.

In this unfamiliar terrain, the cold storms of doubt will rage in our hearts. All we will have is a vague certainty that something better is to come: an inexplicable assurance that a new horizon is near. Of this we become certain because the enlightenment of our awakened consciousness is revealing an inconceivable journey that tears apart our disempowerment. All we can, and must do, is sit with the unknown and allow it to transform us, because the unfamiliar is spirit inviting us to go deeper within, and the discomfort we feel is spirit changing our form.

The onset of our journey is perhaps the most challenging. First, we become aware that to begin, we must choose to say goodbye to our world as we know it. Everything changes. Everything we have created in our lives in the false self will collapse because there is no bearable foundation for a desolate life built on lies.

Ironically, even relinquishing the bad can be difficult when it's all we have ever known. Starting over seems scary. Learning a new way of life appears intimidating. Our limited thinking will make us worry about possible criticism and judgment. It will make us fear rejection. Most of all, it will try to terrify us with thoughts that we may not be strong enough to endure the process of change.

As we begin to shift our lives, our lies collide with our truth, and everything seems at odds with each other—this happens because we are breaking away from our past by exposing the lies and overpowering them with our truth. The unfamiliar truth challenges the familiar that is built on a lie.

We will confront our brokenness but learn that we are the source of our strength. We will face our darkness but discover that we are the light that illuminates our path. We will feel confused but know that our answers lie within. We will feel pain but will know healing. We will feel torn down but will begin to rise. With every step we take, we will battle the demons of the past, but we also will discover our greatness.

The more frequently we journey within, the more the comfort of our familiarity will become our greatest discomfort, but that familiarity no longer will have the strong pull it once did. We will become rooted in the truth and begin to discover that the resoluteness of our hearts will keep us forging ahead in faith. Still, the questions remain: How do we initiate change? How do we accept that our lives are built on a lie and decide to change that? How do we become a person completely different from the one we have always known? Most importantly, who is this person?

Without knowing it, we grow addicted to the negative thought patterns that govern our minds and the damaging behavior patterns that have taken over our lives and continue the vicious cycle of poisoning our souls. We become addicted to the false self, because it is the only way we learned to cope with the experiences that shamed us and kept our pain buried. We have battled the demons of the past our entire lives: the shame that left us destitute and the pain that crippled us. For our own survival, we built an impenetrable fortress constructed of denial around us. It gave us a temporary refuge, because our pain became barricaded behind those sealed walls, but at the same time, so did our authentic selves.

For us to proceed unwaveringly into our hearts and claim our rightful place in our destinies, we must find the courage to confront the pain that has anguished us. We must overcome any physical, mental, and emotional discouragement that tries to prevent us from breaking down the walls that keep us from living authentically. The very spirit we have entrapped in those walls is the strength we need, the courage we seek, and the self-assurance for which we yearn. If we allow discouragement to deter us from our journeys, we will remain ensnared in a chronic feeling of emptiness, wandering forever in an unforgiving landscape of disillusion.

Nothing outside us can define us. If we want to realize the life we desire, we need to look at the person in the mirror and see who it reflects. If we don't like what we see, we need to make a choice and change it; the power lies within us. There is no greater power outside us. We must reclaim the power we have relinquished to our past and the false beliefs that have hindered us from discovering our authentic selves. We hold the answers we have been seeking. We are the light for which we have been searching. We are the destiny we have been pursuing. We are the gift for which we have been waiting. We must let go and look ahead, because in the absence of everything, there is only you, the spirit of your being. You are the answer, the authentic self.

Part I

When Calls the Heart

The Invitation

Pain has its own narrative, but it is only part of our history and not our full story. Sometimes it can feel inescapable because we keep repeating the same narrative with different characters. I was so familiar with the narrative of my pain that it became louder than the language of my heart, love. Pain was louder than love to such a degree that I mistook it for love. But love doesn't hurt; only pain does, and I was hurting.

I remember all too clearly the moment pain grabbed hold of me like a great force of nature. It felt like a tsunami unleashing its fury, and I was drowning in great torrents of emotions that came crashing in on me. Every ounce of pain I suppressed in my depths, hoping to confine it to a black hole in a corner of my unconscious, was unleashed suddenly with all its might.

It was an evening of perfect weather, but an unexpected storm shook the foundation of my core, and its already flawed structure began to crumble.

I recall running down the stairs, and the voice behind me got louder and louder, and my pace quickened. "I hate you. I hate you. I hate you. I hate you!" I heard him say, his voice rising frantically each time he uttered the words. I was looking for a place to escape his rage. The words felt like scorching heat breathing down the back of my neck, but I moved fast. I knew the anger in that voice all too well.

I ran down the stairs desperately, went into the bathroom, and locked myself in. Already in tears, I wrapped my arms around my shaking body and dropped to the floor, overtaken by fear. Maybe if I was out of his sight, he would calm down—at least that's what my naive mind thought. But a shadow overtook the sliver of light coming in through the bottom of the door, and I heard his steps charging in my direction. As the steps came closer and became louder, my fear took away my breath, and panic overcame me. I started to hyperventilate, but the sudden pounding on the door was like thunder that paralyzed me.

Seconds felt like an eternity. Everything turned into a haze. Every hateful word killed my spirit a little more until I became numb. The haze began to pass, and his words became clearer. "I hate you. You're not worth anything." His words became too hurtful to bear; our relationship had become a manifesto of all my past trauma. So, just like that, I shut the window to the world, until it was just me, like a thousand times before.

I wasn't crying. I wasn't hyperventilating. I wasn't scared. I listened again intently, but I could feel my chest crushing against my beating heart with every dreadful word. And again, there was no room to breathe. Then, I stopped listening. I leaned on my side slowly until I was lying on the cold tiles of the bathroom floor, my face grateful for the coolness that soothed my tired, tear-stained face. There was nowhere to go, except to my familiar place, a place in mind so far from reality pain couldn't reach it.

When painful experiences became the norm in my early childhood, to cope, I wandered off into a dreamlike state. To escape the nightmare of my reality, I dreamed. Nothing in my dream world was real; in that world, I was loved. Being loved was my deepest yearning; not surprisingly, it became my familiar place. I created that place in the darkness of my innocence.

That day on the bathroom floor, I grieved with pain like many times before, but that time I couldn't escape to my familiar place, no matter how much I tried. Instead, my mind wandered to those dark days of my childhood, and I remembered everything that led me to that cold floor. I could see me clearly. I was thinking of my childhood victimization.

My head rested on my shoulder, looking in the direction of my outstretched arm, and my eyes caught a glimpse of the doll staring at my fingertips. I opened my eyes wide for a brief second and wiggled my fingertips. I couldn't reach it, but I didn't stop. I would close my eyes and wander off with my innocence and imagined magic, until magic happened. In that real-life nightmare, I created a dream. In my dream state, I played princess with my doll, and I didn't have to look down and see how I was violated again and again. I could numb myself, and I didn't have to feel the touches that scarred my body with emotional wounds that terrorized me with great agony. I avoided the eyes that pierced at me with evil and strangled my heart with fear. In my place, for that time, I could ignore the voice that would later haunt my dreams, because in my body someone decided to bury the sins of their soul and leave me to relive the horrors of every encounter for years to come.

That stormy day, someone else was firing the hellish cycle that began during my childhood. My life mirrored the pain that never healed. As I lay on the floor, a sudden spurt of his yelling brought me back to reality, along with the pain of the past, meshed in the pain of the present. Everything became a frightening haze I couldn't see my way out of. The pain wasn't letting me breathe, and I could feel myself suffocating.

He kept yelling, and I started to wonder, *Will he get to me? What will it be like this time around? Will he sweep across the floors with me again? Will he bang my head into the walls again? Or will it be worse this time?*

I was so scared, and the pain was too much to endure. The words he spoke were cutting to the heart of me, and his rage was igniting a fear that paralyzed me. I began to shut down again, but then he walked away, and something far more frightening started to happen.

Hearing him walk away hurt me more than his words, and the silence that followed scared me more than his anger. I realized later, I would have rather had a love that hurt than no love at all, and he couldn't have hated me more than I hated myself, but it was the only love language I had ever known.

Everything became still, and time seemed to pass slowly, but I managed to numb myself until I felt nothing. Still, the pain was raging in me like a simmering volcano, and eventually more memories of my childhood erupted. I felt betrayed by my heart, but truth has no escape. This was only the beginning.

I reached a point when I doubted all that I was and feared all that I might never be. I grew tired of living in the perplexity produced by doubt and fear. Happiness seemed more like a distant mirage created to tease me, almost torture me, because it seemed so unattainable. My hope became outweighed by despair. I started to believe that I should conform to what was, rather than hope for what could be, but the intriguing mystery and the limitless possibilities of what could be wouldn't escape me. Relentlessly, I asked myself the same questions repeatedly: Is there more to life than just pain? Could happiness be real? Am I more than just my victimization? Can I heal and know true love? I had started to convince myself to stop yearning for more and stop asking questions for which I thought I'd probably never find the answers, but my questions weighed heavily on me. I longed for nothing more than the answer to my questions. To my great fortune, my heart's desire proved to be greater than the emotional fatigue that weighed on me, so I kept in search of my truth.

My turning point came in the most unforeseen moment; at the time I didn't know it, but the moment would mark a crucial point in my life.

One day, a friend invited me to an event designed for women in leadership. In all honesty, I didn't want to attend, but the woman who invited me was a good friend, and I didn't want to disappoint her. She seemed excited about organizing this gathering for her close friends, women she hand-selected for this "life-changing affair," so I attended reluctantly, thinking it would be far from life changing—but little did I know. I won't go into all the specifics of the event, just the moment that steered my life in a new direction.

There we were, all the attendees sitting around the conference table, discussing our careers, talking about our goals, and sharing why we chose to attend the event. Suddenly, in the distant murmuring, I heard the words that brought the conversation in the room to an abrupt halt, "What is your mission statement for life?" At first, I wasn't sure whether I had heard correctly. My attention refocused on the speaker who asked that riveting, fateful question once again, "Could anyone in the crowd tell me your mission statement for life?" I wasn't mistaken, and to my surprise, the words rattled my core.

As she asked again, the words crashed into me like the iceberg that sank the great *Titanic*. I wasn't prepared for that question. I was expecting typical questions, such as: What are your goals? What professional aspirations do you have? But that wasn't the question, and I didn't have an answer. I could feel her question piercing me as I sank into my chair, hoping the cataclysmic collapse that was occurring in my being would go unnoticed. I was in sheer panic. There I was, struggling with myself. "What was my mission statement for life?" I simply didn't know.

I didn't understand why the words struck me with the force of crashing waves that destroyed every layer of my defenses in a matter of seconds. My reasoning failed me, my logic betrayed me, and my intelligence was useless. Unexpectedly, my body responded as if it were under attack. My flight-or-fight response was activated, and I prepared instinctively for a fight. Then, in an instant, every sense in my being was activated in the hope of answering that one question as if my life depended on it.

Nothing made any sense. I found that I had two choices. I could choose to ignore what was happening and continue in my familiar patterns, or I could choose the unfamiliar territory ahead. Life is birthed in the choices we make in a split second.

When we want something different in life, sometimes the way to obtain it makes no sense at all. Reasoning, logic, and intelligence fail us in life-altering moments, because we are trying something we have never tried before. When life presents us with these moments, we must have the courage to listen to our heart minds and be willing to be uncomfortable in the unfamiliar. I've come to recognize that I'm on the right path in these moments of great discomfort, because it means I am on the road less travelled.

Have you ever heard the expression, "Think with your heart"? Maybe, more often than not you've heard, "Don't think with your heart." Well, in my experience, that is for people who cannot break through the walls of familiarity and find the courage to be uncomfortable in the unfamiliar. Your heart will always guide you in ways that contradict reason, challenge logic, and defy intelligence. But the heart of you is the only path to living out your destiny.

That day, I chose the unfamiliar path, and in a second, I changed the entire course of my life. Still, it did not stop me from trying to find reason, from trying to find logic, from trying to intellectualize the events. My choice didn't enable me magically to fight my discomfort and make me immune to unfamiliarity. There I was; it was like a storm raging inside me; it was the battle between my false self and the authentic self. Soon, fear would try to overtake me, a natural response to the familiar that felt threatened. I couldn't comprehend fully what was happening. However, something far more powerful than my fear gripped me, so when I couldn't comprehend it, I stopped trying to. Instead, I did instinctively what came next and channeled my courage to experience it. I became fully present in the now. And with that choice, my heart began to operate fully—it was an act of courage, and courage is not of the mind but of the heart. And so I gave birth to the life compass that guided me to my turning point.

That day, I wrote my mission statement for life: *to be the most powerful expression of my authentic self.* It was a powerful declaration. I felt like life was inviting me on a journey within, into the heart of me, and I accepted the invitation.

I was ready to heal.

First Insight

The heart is the gatekeeper of the authentic self.

Be willing to take the journey within.

We Are Spiritual Beings Having a Human Experience

Spirit is infinite. We will never know its truth. Our finite brain minds could not even begin to conjure an explanation that could come close to it. Truth is the unadulterated authenticity of a being, the purest expression of its divine existence.

Spirit is one. It is whole, perfect, and complete. It is not differentiated by forms of existence; spirit *is* existence. Therefore, it is in everything that exists, and everything that exists is an expression of spirit. We exist because spirit lives in us, and therefore, we are spirit having a human experience. We are the unique expression of its perfection, wholeness, and completeness.

My definition of the heart mind is the part of us where science ends and our divinity begins: spirit. Life in our mind derives from the connection between our physical being and the external world. The life of our heart mind derives from the connection between our heart and our spirit. Without the brain mind, there is no expression of our human experience. But without heart, there is no life, and life is the expression of our divine existence: spirit.

When we lose our connection to spirit, life becomes only the expression of our human experience. For our brain mind to function, it must be sustained by our external world, like the oxygen we breathe. But for our heart mind to function, it must be sustained by our internal being—our unadulterated truth that is perfect, whole, and complete in the authentic self.

Our spiritual being cannot alter its truth, and therefore it cannot change its authenticity. Spirit is. Spirit is perfect; therefore, it cannot be shamed. For this reason, it doesn't know the dishonor caused by abuse, neglect, and abandonment. Spirit is whole; therefore, it cannot be broken, and so it doesn't know the devastation caused by agony, sorrow, and despair. Spirit is complete; therefore, it cannot be destitute, and hence it doesn't know the unworthiness caused by insecurities, guilt, and judgment. Spirit operates only by truth, the authenticity of its existence.

Conversely, our human experience can only alter our brain mind, which is made up of a collection of information gathered from our interactions with our external world and the way in which we experience them in our physical beings. What we live and what we learn from our external world generates a physical response that is happening concurrently, and our brain stores the sum of the experiences and creates memory.

Memories are crucial to our existence, as they influence our decisions in the present. Memories formed from experiences in early childhood, experiences that were traumatic, and the frequency of these experiences, play a key role in our lives. Memories shape our perception of the world and alter our realities. More importantly, memories can veil the truth about us through ourselves.

It is not easy to accept that our past is just a memory and not our reality. Some of us become stuck living in our memories and make present decisions accordingly. The danger comes when our memories are traumatic experiences rooted deeply in our physical, mental, and emotional bodies. Unless we uproot and heal the pain embedded in those memories, our decisions will create a perpetual cycle of the past.

When our present begins to look like our past, we become

convinced that the sum of our reality is our traumatic experiences. Breaking that link between our present and the memories rooted in past trauma allows us to rip the veil and unlock the potential of discovering our truth, so we can live it.

The Journey with the Heart

Reflection I: The Road Less Travelled

Journeying into the heart of us is the road less travelled. As it appears, this road is always the one to choose, but it rarely is the one *we* choose. Now I know and understand why. Journeying into the self was one of my most difficult choices. Before I anchored where I am today, I set out to accomplish serious goals. I designed a journey so far out of myself that I'm not sure I would have ever found myself. But as destiny would have it, the journey on which I embarked was full of experiences and people that helped me find my true destiny. By destiny, I mean me.

You see, nothing happens by mere coincidence. At any given moment, we all are designing our destinies. All our thoughts manifest an external physical counterpart that reflects the state of our inner beings. The state of my inner being was a deep yearning to realize my destiny. I was desperate to answer the ageless question that has brought complete fulfillment to some people who have been able to find the answer and great grief to the many who go through life without ever knowing it: *who am I and what is my purpose?*

Although I didn't know it then, every external experience was designed to help me find the answer. I spent years reading books, listening to inspiring lectures and motivational speakers, and visiting religious temples in search of my truth. I hoped that someone or something could help me discover who I am and my destiny. For me, that was the key to happiness. In my ignorance, I believed that happiness was the ultimate destiny, so I did everything to arrive at that destination. Although I learned later that I was operating under false beliefs, for a time, the desire to achieve happiness was my driving force, and later I came to see it as my saving grace because every event in my life led me to that crossroads where eventually I had to choose between my false self and authentic self.

Reflection II: Turning Point

A life force within me led me to the moment that inspired my mission statement for life, my turning point.

Not long after, I realized I had not only written the mission statement for my life, but I had written my destiny. The panic I had felt subsided and turned into hope for a new way of life. From that moment on, I had one goal and one goal alone, to fulfill my mission statement by living accordingly. There would be no deviation, and conformity was not an option. In that moment, I became single-minded. I had written my truth, and I would live by it and let destiny unfold.

I recognize now that my reluctance to attend the event existed only in my mind, where reason, logic, and intellect failed me. However, there was an inner self that operated differently, and it was forever willing. My decision to attend came from that part of us we can't quite understand but irrefutably know exists. We channel it through our heart mind. It is the ultimate guide to our greater self.

Our heart mind is powerful. It helps us channel hope and faith. It fuels our tenacity, determination, drive, and perseverance. It is the energy that helps us overcome our barriers and achieve our greatness. Even if we cannot understand or define it fully, we know it has an unequivocal force that holds the key to our fullest potential.

Reflection III: The Heart Mind

I mentioned earlier that at any given moment, we are designing our destiny. I believe that the greater force in our being is all-powerful and all-knowing, and it is always conspiring on our behalf to direct us to our destiny.

There is no science that can explain this part of human matter fully. It remains indefinable. It is as much a mystery as the beginning of humankind. But like the many theories that have evolved to explain the beginning of life, much has evolved to explain this undeniable source of life. However, unlike the life generated by our physical bodies that science continues to try to explain, this unequivocal force of our human nature remains a great mystery. For the purposes of this book, I simply distinguish our brain mind from our heart mind.

The course of our lives is directed by the processes in the entity we know as the mind. The mind is where thought and emotion live. It is a complex nature that cannot be explained fully by any one entity. However, the functions associated most closely with the mind are the functions of the brain and the functions of the heart, two of the most complex organs in our bodies. Although the sum of it all remains a great mystery, it is the heart that we have associated with great immeasurable matters that lead to one universal truth and the most powerful source of life: love.

It is my philosophy that the heart mind is where science ends and our divinity begins. To become aware of this fully is the greatest paradigm shift of all. In honor of my truth, it is the journey to the heart of me that led me to discover my authentic self, and in that journey, I discovered the greatest love of all. Knowing oneself is to love oneself. I can only hope that we may all have the courage to journey within in search of our truth and live the most powerful version of our authentic selves.

Looking back, I believe I wasn't meant to remember the details of the moment I found myself at the crossroads but to recall instead the catalyst of my turning point, because in that moment, I birthed my truth. Sometimes, the most unforeseen moments are the key to opening new gateways in a new direction.

Relinquishing the limitations of my brain mind and connecting to my heart mind to unveil my limitlessness and discover my truth was the paradigm shift that set me free. For too long, I relied on the brain mind, but my reason, logic, and intellect governed and failed me. It was my heart mind that guided me to go within, let go, and go beyond.

Reflection IV: A Pondering Heart

Long before this moment, I wrote a journal entry I later titled, *The Woman in the Mirror*. When I first began to write the entry, I reflected on one of the most tormenting moments of my life, a time when all hope had escaped me, but I endured nonetheless. It was a reminder that I had overcome a great deal, and it was an opportunity to turn the memory into a commemoration that marked hope rather than the hopelessness I once felt.

But after I finished writing, I began to think, *If those things had never happened to me, what would my identity be then? What kind of person would I have become? Did I know who I was outside of that pain?* All that I had become was connected intrinsically to that past, to the girl peering into the mirror of her past. I felt saddened deeply, and in that sadness, a question came to mind that gave life to an idea, an idea that turned into a journey, a journey that became my destiny. What is my authentic self?

I pondered this question for hours until I realized something happened when I asked myself that question, and I understood it would take more than an evening to find the answers. I often wondered how many others struggled with the same thoughts, trying to find who they are outside of the experiences that have come to define them. Thus, I decided to find those answers.

At first, I was in my head and not my heart, so I approached the process logically. I became educated on the subject matter, which was the foundation of a great career, but I found no answers. I did research and tried to understand my trauma through science, but it only raised more questions. I partook in religions and rituals, but I was more confused than ever. I attended conferences and seminars, but I mastered only my craft, and in the meantime, I was decompensating slowly. I spent many futile years looking for answers and finding none.

Every search led me to an even greater search so far outside of myself that I became lost in my own quest. During that part of my journey, I became successful but remained unfulfilled. I was popular but lonely, surrounded with awards and accolades but with broken relationships and a void that consumed me. Still, there are no coincidences in life. This doesn't minimize my great epiphany; it amplifies it. After I exhausted my search outside myself, I was left only with the journey within.

There were many great lessons I needed to learn. Every experience taught me that the answers weren't outside me; they were within, and that became clear to me the moment I connected to my heart mind.

Our heart mind is always guiding us; we simply need to learn to identify it and be one with it. With every breath we take, we pump life into our brain mind, but with every pump of our heart mind, we bring life to our divinity, that indefinable force I call spirit. In my spirit, I had always known the answers; I just needed to take the journey within.

Reflection V: A Survivor's Journey into the Authentic Self

We are mind, body, and spirit. Fulfillment comes when the sum of all parts forms a harmonious whole in the expression of the authentic self. The authentic self is the purest manifestation of the self and is perfect, whole, and complete. Our authenticity is our truth. My truth is expressed uniquely through me, just as yours is expressed uniquely through you; it is a truth that can be discovered only by going within. When life presents us with an invitation to go within, with each step we take into our heart, we peel away the layers that separate us from our greatness, because in the end, the illusory walls of pain from the past are annihilated, and the imaginary fear of the future is shattered. Then, all we have left is the gift of the present, the unadulterated expression of our most powerful being, the authentic self.

Part II

Revelations of the Heart

The Woman in the Mirror

I once stood before a young woman who was on the verge of ending her life. I stared into her eyes and watched as she drowned herself in tears of pain, shame, and hurt. She looked directly into my eyes, and I felt the weight of her helplessness and confusion. She cried out in desperation, asking for an explanation why her life had been filled with so much anguish. She thought about the nightmares that were her constant nocturnal companions and did not allow her to forget. She remembered waking up in rumpled, sweaty sheets, feeling the cold, gripping fingers of her memories as they violated her again and again; the cold tentacles of terror that came over her each time she relived the agony of being dishonored, every disgusting touch and every brutal strike. Although she held up her hands to cover her ears, she could still hear every dreadful word ever spoken to her, the voices echoing in the emptiness of her hollow heart. Regardless of how many tears she shed, they couldn't wash away the suffering of her soul. The weight of abuse became unbearable and too much for her to carry alone.

The woman I saw was me, peering into a mirror.

For as long as I can recollect, my life was a whirlwind of turmoil, in which I lived each moment in downward spirals, frantically running from the pain in my past while destroying my future. So, I did what many of us do; I tried to design a destiny that could give my pain purpose.

For a time, it almost worked. My professional success had me convinced that I had transformed my pain into something meaningful, but all the success in the world couldn't heal the wounds that were festering in my core. All I truly accomplished was finding a way to live with my pain rather than releasing it.

In the end, I was sucked into the turmoil. My life came crashing in, and one hard look in the mirror gave me the chance to face my pain at last before it stole my last breath of life.

Second Insight

Truth is the unadulterated expression of the authentic self.

Be willing to look in the mirror until you can see
beyond the deception and recognize your truth.

The Authentic Self versus the False Self

The arrangement of our DNA marks each of us in a way so unique that no human being is alike, just as the mark of our fingerprints. In the same way, spirit imprints on us in a manner so unique that no two human beings can be alike. Our "spirit print" is found in our authenticity. However, when our human experiences overpower our divinity, our authentic self is compromised.

I mentioned earlier that we are spiritual beings having a human experience. Our spirit is the power of our being, the essence of our existence. Spirit permeates us by our mere existence. The gift of our divinity is without repentance—we are the unique expression of spirit. However, when we don't channel our most powerful self in our authenticity, a compromised self evolves—a false self.

The false self is the shadow of our authentic self. It seeks to be what the authentic self is. Yet, by its very nature, it can never know true fulfillment. The false self relies primarily on the brain mind and seeks to find destiny externally. It succeeds based upon accomplishments, thus altering destiny to be something to be obtained or achieved. Our personal, professional, and social fulfillment become matters of success to be compared and measured, limiting our personal, professional, and social success to our human experiences and the knowledge we obtain throughout. Nevertheless, you can be a great success in every area of your life but never live authentically, have a perfect, whole, and complete life, and experience true fulfillment. Conversely, the authentic self relies on the heart mind and knows that its most powerful expression is our destiny, which is found only within.

It is much easier to see through the veil of despair than the veil of success. Despair can be unbearable, but it doesn't deceive you; it reveals itself in its truest form, while success is a deceitful instrument that perpetuates the denial of the authentic self. However, when we are not living purposeful lives through authentic living, lack of fulfillment is sure to seep in like venom; slowly, but surely, a great void will cast its shadow over our lives, and the constant search to fill that void will become our unrest. The need for self-acceptance will drive our desire for more success. Nonetheless, even the greatest success amounts only to a vain attempt for self-acceptance, because success requires the validation of the external world. Validation of oneself can never be sustained by another, and the attempt itself becomes a vicious cycle of self-destruction. Real validation is the unadulterated acceptance of the self.

However, facing the false self in the depths of despair or at the heights of success can be equally difficult, because you must come face-to-face with your truth. To do so, you must unmask the false self and peel away the layers of deception until you expose the depths of shame that inundate you and the heights of the walls of denial that shield you from your pain.

This is the moment of truth: when we allow ourselves to be moved in the direction of our authenticity. We must trust that we are rooted in truth and allow our hearts to be our northern star in discovering a new world within.

The Journey with Truth

Reflection I: The Mirror of Truth

There I lay, in a bed of lies, facing my false self. I had no idea how to begin to rise from the emotional abyss in which I had been living for so long. However, one thing was certain: facing my truth spared me no anguish. The pain of my past was surfacing unapologetically, and all the suffering that had created my fears flared without mercy. Suddenly, I was overwhelmed with panic. The pain in the eyes of the woman in the mirror was unforgiving. Nevertheless, I was ready to confront my demons.

An audacious hope brewed and stirred deep inside my being the moment I connected to my heart mind, and in the desperation of my despair, I began to believe. Nonetheless, when you have abandoned yourself to the fate of the false self, there is no way to escape your demons on your journey back. I had to make a choice. I could remain in the false self and continue to live my life in the shadow of myself, buried in shame and armored in denial, or I could gird myself in hope and trust the process. It was my choice, and with only a sliver of hope, I chose to delve within and stood steadfast looking at the woman in the mirror.

There is no guide when you choose to go within and face the demons that have tormented you every step of the way, but there is light in the hope. I saw very little of that light, but it was sufficient to grasp the belief that my light would be greater than my darkness. However, the only way to turn my belief into my truth was to stop running and face my darkness.

Reflection II: Discovering the Light Within

Once again, I was shaken to the core and broken by the deception unfolding before my eyes. Once again, I existed in a place of debilitating pain, the kind that sears your soul and leaves you feeling lifeless. I wasn't simply going through the motions of drowning in a sea of emotions; I was dying. Except I was alive, and that is what hurt me the most.

It was a pain like that of a slow death, which leaves you gasping for air, but taking another breath keeps you holding on for longer than you can bear. I couldn't help but think to myself, *Could this be it? Is this all there is to life, pain and more pain? Hurt and more hurt, sadness and more sadness?* My thoughts raced until an overwhelming number of fleeting thoughts took me into the darkest place in my being to wonder in anguish, *If this is all life has to offer, is it worth moving forward? Or would it be easier to give up? After all, who wants to live in a constant internal battle with pain and all its misery?* My questions didn't improve from there, but instead they began to debate matters of life and death.

I wish I could say that moment was my lowest and my weakest, but it wasn't. I was standing in my familiar place, with a deep longing to die. I was facing the darkness that had been taunting me for years. I didn't know it then, but I realized later that I never truly wanted to die. Somehow, though, I had found something soothing in the thoughts suspended between life and death. I felt solace imagining an end to my pain, because I simply couldn't fathom any other escape from the events of my past.

The deeper I looked within, the less anything made sense. For the first time, I was peering into the heart of me, but at first all I could see was my ravished soul. Denial was losing its grip, and as the walls of illusion crumbled around me, there came revelation. Finally, my shame and pain were exposed. I felt that I lived my life on crutches that helped support my handicapped soul. Still, as the shame in me began to be unmasked and the layers of pain began to be peeled away, I felt like I was being suffocated by the stranglehold of fear.

My light of hope was dimmed suddenly by the waves of emotions that enveloped me. The darkness was daunting. For a long time, I had wrapped myself in denial as strong as armor. It was the key to my survival, and I didn't know how to survive without it. When I decided finally to face my truth and stood to look at the woman in the mirror, nothing could conceal my pain or hide my unworthiness. I was suddenly completely vulnerable.

I had more questions than ever. Torn between my past and my future, at that moment, all I could do was cry. I would sink into a pool of my tears and cry for help, but nothing happened. I felt abandoned but not by others. I felt abandoned by myself, like I had given up the only thing that sustained me: my false self.

Denial is one of the most powerful coping mechanisms. It helps us hide our pain so we can continue with our lives and never face what is hidden directly in our core. However, living in denial is like building a glass house; it can weather some storms, but eventually the pain will strike and shatter it. When that time comes, we are left with nothing but the broken pieces to clean up.

At the time, I had no idea what was next. I didn't know what awaited me after this sudden awakening. However, I felt my slumbering spirit rising and a storm beginning to rage inside me. I was facing the pain that defined my life and the immeasurable fear I had of releasing it. The two charged at me with an unforgiving force in a relentless fight to remain. Yet something else was happening. An equally great force had been awakened. I couldn't begin to comprehend the nature of it, but somehow I knew that the storm needed to rage on. My hope gave me faith; it wasn't a mountain-moving faith, but it was faith nonetheless, and with faith came trust.

For the first time, rather than leaning on my fear, I anchored myself in faith and trusted the process would prevail. I didn't think about how, but in my heart, I knew that in my greatest darkness, I had discovered my light, because in that moment, I chose to be present with everything in my being.

Every great journey begins with a single first step, and choosing to be present was my first step.

Reflection III: Awakened

I had stepped into the unknown, living with my eyes wide open. I had my mission statement of life, and I was determined to live it. From that moment forward, I continued to journey into the heart of me. I wish I could say this made everything easier, but it didn't. I had faced my darkness, but now I had to face the life I had constructed and had to learn to build a new life anchored in my truth.

I had built a life based on false beliefs about myself, and the deeper I went within, the more the lies were unmasked. I never had a greater sense of loss. I didn't know how to be authentically me, but I didn't want to be who I had become, and that desire began to grow until it became greater than the need to cling to my pain.

It was not a simple process, as the more I looked within, the more I realized I couldn't see myself. But I also could not see the woman I had created for the world: the woman who hid her pain behind a smile, her unworthiness in good deeds, and her vulnerabilities in success. The layers that crippled my authenticity, hidden in shame, brokenness, and unworthiness, were beginning to peel away.

As I began to discover my truth, I became aware that my false self was defined by a past that weighed on me heavily. It was full of wounds that had never healed. Its pain was embodied in an endless agonizing torture of unworthiness and sadness, buried in sorrow and grief.

My circumstances and relationships were constant reminders of my past. I kept repeating the same cycle of pain. I realized that I had become dependent on my present experiences to recreate the past in a desperate attempt to change the outcome and rewrite the ending. I thought maybe I finally would have the chance to annihilate my past pain. However, the past cannot be rewritten, and the present is a gift that allows us to start over. I didn't see that then, because I was blinded. My vision was veiled by my false self, while my authentic self continued to slumber. However, as my spirit awakened, so did my courage to continue my journey into my authentic self.

One would think this was hardly a glorious beginning. But in fact, it was! The thing about birthing new life is that first you feel nothing but pain. Until this point, denial was like a bandage placed securely over my past, which hurt too much to tear off because I was afraid to see what lay underneath.

At first, I couldn't understand why I had to revisit the pain I had been running from for so long. Yet I could no longer deny that the source of my pain was the wounds of my past that had never healed. They had remained open, and I continued to relive each time my innocence had been ravished, every brutal strike that marked my essence, and every dreadful word that pierced my heart. To heal, it was inevitable that I needed to revisit my wounds. Denial kept me running from my pain, and that's how I survived. However, it was time to stop running. I knew how to survive, but I needed to learn to overcome. My identity was absorbed in my need to survive, but being a survivor only proves that you can endure pain, while being someone who overcomes proves that you are worthy of something much more than pain.

Reflection IV: Audacious Hope

For most of my life, my thoughts were entangled in the memories abandoned by the light of day, where only darkness dwelled, mixed with the cold mist of my tears. In that place, I met with a toddler who was abused sexually before she could even begin to understand why her body was being used for such purposes. At other times, it was a little girl crushed by the emotional neglect she had endured before her legs could reach the floor from the chair of the kitchen table. Often, however, it was a rude encounter with the girl who daydreamed of becoming a beautiful young woman, but the scars of the physical abuse and the horror of being raped mercilessly before she was sweet sixteen left little to dream about. Instead, life seemed like one eternal nightmare from which she could not awaken.

I have seen the force of a fist, every blow in close proximity, before shutting the windows of the world and locking me in a dark abyss for seconds, sometimes minutes, and then all over again, until his anger consumed my fragile, beaten body completely. I have conversed with my silent companion, the brisk, cold air when I was homeless, living out of my car, wandering aimlessly. I have danced with death each time I summoned it. Yes, I called it. I made sweet love to it, but each dance left me on the floor between worlds with a broken compass, not dead but not quite alive.

I thought to myself, *If not by death, how can I escape the nightmares that come unannounced? And where can I bury my pain?* I have seen my life buried in the bloodstained sidewalk that marked where my brother was murdered. If not death, what could make my memories fade into the abyss of the forgotten? My heartaches were like a cancer that ate away at me. These were some of the events that made me a prisoner of war, a war that shattered the grounds of the present and trapped me in the agony of the past as I relived my story again and again. There were different characters, but it was the same old storyline.

What do you do after you have been ravished by a legion of darkness? And what comes next, after you've been shattered into a million pieces? When the air you breathe becomes thin and your mind clouds, where do you find solace?

In a place where pain has no substitute and there seems to be no comfort for your wounds, how do you begin to heal? When a drum line of anxiety crowds your morning thoughts and the sound of a godforsaken melody beats against your hollow heart at night, can pain ever know peace?

The answer was simply *yes*. Somehow, in the heart of me, I always knew. Despite pain's iron grip, an unblemished belief blossomed in my heart, telling me that there was something greater than the pain. The betrayal of my mind is what kept me living in my pain. I relived it over and over again, trying to make sense of it, trying to explain it, and each time, I failed to overcome it and continued to be overcome by it instead.

Reflection V: Overpowering the Darkness

The word *healing* can be misleading. We think of healing, and our minds wander off automatically to soothing images. At least my mind does! I think of fluffy pillows, warm comforters, and the aroma of sweet herbal tea—and if we are lucky, someone will be at our side nursing us back to health. However, there is no comfort or sweet aroma associated with healing from the wounds of our past, and for the most part, it's a process we must endure alone.

Healing needs to follow its natural course. It will cause distress, it will create discomfort, and it will hurt. Resisting the process only amplifies the pain. Healing a wounded soul has only one remedy— you must feel the pain.

When a physical wound is left untreated, it becomes infected, and we need to be ready for this because the healing will hurt far more than the initial injury. The process of healing an infected wound won't begin before the infection that has plagued our body is remedied first. In the same manner, when we leave the wounds of our heart untreated, they also become infected and plague our spirits rather than our bodies. Our core becomes diseased with false beliefs that manifest in shame, fear, insecurities, bitterness, resentment, and more. Before we can heal, we must uproot every unhealthy belief that has created our false self.

That was my situation. I had left my wounds untreated for so long that my pain flared at every opportunity. Nevertheless, I had begun the process of healing. Healing doesn't mean the wounds never existed; it simply means they no longer have power over us.

My spirit had awakened from its slumber, and I could see a new horizon. I felt a storm raging inside me, but I continued my journey because my light would soon overpower my darkness.

Part III

A Wailing Heart

The Course of Pain

That day, behind the locked bathroom door- pain took its course.

I remember recalling the year 1983- I was begging and pleading desperately—

"Look at me, please. Talk to me. I'm sorry. I'm so sorry. I won't do it again. I love you. Please look at me. I promise I won't do it again. Talk to me, please. Please say something. Talk to me. I love you! —I love you!"

I remembered crying and begging as my fragile six-year-old body fell to its knees in tears. I remembered sobbing, kissing her feet for forgiveness, and laying my chest on her feet as I wrapped my skinny arms around her ankles and held on in pure desperation, waiting for a response, waiting for a reaction, waiting for her to say something, anything. I cried desperately for an "I love you too" or an "It's okay. I forgive you." But eventually, my crying exhausted my little girl's strength, so that a nod or even a look my way would have been enough. Anything, a single gesture or word, would have been enough. And sometimes it was. It wasn't an isolated incident. Sometimes, after what seemed like an eternity, a shrug away or a scream to shut me up became enough because it made me feel like I was there; she knew that I was there. Anything was better than her stone-cold, emotionless face turned away from me. A push or a scream let me know I was there. I never did anything to deserve the treatment I received; I just thought I did, as it was the only thing that made sense to me. I felt punished. I was only a child, and I didn't know why I wasn't loved.

But years later, there I was again—begging to be loved. "Why don't you love me?" These were the only words I could utter while lying on the floor. My mind was fogged, and my reality was clouded. I couldn't distinguish the pain from my past and the pain from the present. Each word he uttered in that present moment was like a key that unlocked the pain I denied—the pain of years of memories sealed in an impenetrable abyss. I never wanted to revisit my memories because the pain connected to them was so excruciating. However, on this day, my pain was unapologetic.

Suddenly, I was startled by a bang on the door, followed by a scream, "Come out!" he demanded. But I did nothing. Once again, thoughts from the past flooded my mind, and the demon I was so afraid to face appeared in my memory. She was ruthless; her cruelty went beyond my mental, emotional, and physical body. The degree to which she allowed my innocence to be ravished repeatedly, with an audience, was the most heinous of all pain any child could suffer. But there she was, vivid. I could still remember the evil in her eyes and the smirk she wore like a trophy, knowing she managed to deceive all who entrusted her with our innocent souls. I feared the terror of these memories the most, but in that moment, the banging on the door and the yelling outside the door transported me to my darkest days, and I began to relive the vilest times of my childhood.

I could remember being shoved into a dark closet, curling up in a fetal position, and listening intently to the voice that terrorized me. "Stay in there, you little whore! And don't come out until I say so!" The door slammed. "Don't come out of the closet. If you do, you know what will happen to you!" My heart raced uncontrollably in the pitch darkness. Mute with fear, I dared not say a word. I was startled as the door swung open with force. "Did you hear me!" I only managed to look up and let the terror in my eyes speak for me as I stared at a face contorted with a wicked laughter. "Oh, you stupid little girl." Approaching me, she grabbed hold of my arm as the horror continued. "You better keep your mouth shut, you hear me?" I nodded and let my eyes sink to my wounded heart. "Look at me! Do you hear me?" I nodded yes. Her laughter was more intense now. "You're nothing but a clown. Come, you want to see?" My body was yanked from the corner floor of the closet and dragged across the floor, coming to a stop at a couch near the bolted door that led outside that hell. "What are you staring at? You think someone is coming to get you? Come here!" Resigned to obey, I stood there, waiting for what would come next. "Let's put this on you." Blood-red lipstick was pressed on my lips, repeatedly, until it was smudged all over my face. "Look!" I stared at myself in the mirror held in front of me. "What do you see? A clown, right? You see a clown, right?" Silenced by fear, my body could only whisper with a shrug of the shoulders as my head pulled into my chest by the weight of my tears. "Look at yourself. I want you to look at yourself and see the clown that you are!" No one was barging through the door to rescue me, but by the time I raised my eyes to look again, numbness had come to my rescue. I stared at myself in the mirror, and I saw the clown. It depicted an image of my innocence washed away in ridicule and humiliation. My eyes were haunted by darkness, and my smile was stolen by pain. Every stain of that bloody lipstick drawn across my face bled my innocence away. I stood there, facing myself in the mirror, paralyzed. "Look at you! You like it? You like the way you look? What are you doing just staring at yourself! You like being a clown? Is that what it is? You piece of shit! I'll teach you to be a clown! Go back and lock yourself in the closet!" I didn't resist. I simply obeyed without hesitation and walked back into the closet. This time, the closet wasn't so scary; the voice behind me was far scarier to endure, and there were far worse things she would have me do that raped every shred of innocence in my body. I was fine with the closet. I could hide there, and I didn't have to hear her direct my virtue being stolen from me. "Look at you. You like it. You see, I'm not doing anything bad. You like it in there, right?" I kept walking. As I walked toward it, it felt like more of a refuge than the dark, scary place I had been terrified of moments before. I shut the door behind me and shut away the voice.

A loud bang brought me back to the present. It was all too familiar; there I was again on the floor, shutting out the voice of pain behind a door.

That moment unsealed what could never be closed again: a path into the heart of me. Pain suffocated me, until it forced me to let life back in.

Third Insight

Pain is the master of deception to the false self but the revealer of truth to the authentic self.

Be willing to sit with your pain, feel your pain, and know your pain until you transform your pain.

Hope in Pain

Pain is the source of all human afflictions, but even the sum of all physical pain could never compare to the mental and emotional agony that can be suffered from wounds. Only spirit is unconquered by pain.

Pain is the agony of a slumbering spirit that is meant to be awakened but isn't because we are too trapped by our human experiences. Such experiences only breed shame, brokenness, and unworthiness, all of which contradict the essence of the authentic self.

The false self emerges from the denial to feel our human afflictions. Living free from pain doesn't mean literally living free from pain. Pain is inevitable; it is part of our human experience. It is as necessary as breathing. Pain serves to protect us, allowing us to know when we are experiencing something that goes against our nature, such as when we have been violated or when our well-being has been compromised.

If we think of physical pain, when we are injured physically, we know to focus and attend to our injury because of the pain in the wound caused by the injury. We know that if the wound is left untreated, it will become infected and cause even greater pain. Similarly, when we are wounded mentally or emotionally, pain brings our attention to that hurt, so we can tend to it. However, many of us simply don't. Unlike physical wounds, mental and emotional wounds often are left unattended, and we continue to feel the agony of the pain. We believe it subsides, but in fact, we only become numb to it.

What we often do instead is deny the pain by engaging in anything external to keep our minds from thinking and our emotions from feeling. However, like breathing, pain is not meant to remain inside us. Every breath gives us life, but the air we breathe must exit before it becomes toxic. Similarly, pain must exit our mental and emotional bodies before it becomes toxic to our being. We are not meant to carry pain. When we do, it poisons us. In the end, we become a shadow of who we were meant to be and not who we were created to be. Nonetheless, pain is relentless, and when it becomes unbearable, the force behind it is the hope of a life without pain.

Spirit doesn't know pain. Therefore, it cannot operate in suffering. The more we fail to tend to our wounds, the longer we allow the pain to linger. The more the venom of pain lingers in our mental and emotional bodies, the more we prevent our authenticity from operating to its fullest potential.

Each day we live denying the present by living in the past, we strengthen the ability of the false self to operate in the shadow of our authentic self. However, the moment we allow spirit to wash away the pain and anchor us in our truth, we know our power and become limitless.

The Journey with Pain

Reflection I: A Heart Full of Pain

I was in Malaysia as part of a global humanitarian tour. While there, I met a woman named Madeleine whose work with victims of sexual abuse I admired greatly, and I volunteered to work with her. We were kindred spirits and connected immediately. Our bond was inevitable; not long after we first met, we spoke of my reasons for being there— my decision to resign everything and embark on such a tour. I went on to explain my love for the cause and told her I was there to help and to raise awareness. However, she asked me the same question again, and again, I explained my reasons. She asked me again and again, until finally I spoke to her about my own victimization and that it was the reason I was passionate about helping prevent others from enduring what I had. I wasn't talking about the victimization itself, but a life trapped in the victimization. Nevertheless, she could see into the heart of me and said, "I think you're here for you."

The words didn't resonate with me immediately. How could they? I had just given up my job security, given away everything I had, and left behind the people I loved to volunteer my time to help victims around the world. I had nothing: not a fancy CEO title, or a luxury car, or an apartment by the Hudson River overlooking the NYC skyline. I had left my friends and my family behind, and she was telling me I was there for me. I was baffled by her words, irritated almost, and all I could say was, "No, I've dealt with my issues. I'm here for the victims."

However, she was a force of nature, and when she knew truth, she would not back down. "I think you're here so you can finally let go of the pain you've been holding onto."

The thing about denial is that it may deceive you, but it doesn't deceive the world. My pain was written all over me, but it took someone who really cared to see it. As she said those words, my walls tumbled down. I didn't have to pretend to be anyone. I didn't even have to pretend to be okay. She was right. I hadn't admitted it to anyone, because that meant having to admit it to myself. But I was in pain, and finally someone looked into the heart of me and said, "I see you, and I see your pain."

I started to cry because I felt confused. I reflected on my journey. I reflected on the pain I was trying to escape, the denial that helped me believe I was fine, the ingenuous belief that my journey would bring me fulfillment—but it didn't. I kept running away from my pain and crashing right into more. To the world, my actions seemed selfless. People used words such as *courageous* and *brave*. "You're my hero, Evelyn," some people told me. But none of those words ever resonated with me. I didn't have peace. In fact, it was my hopelessness that made me give it all up. I named my mission Project HOPE 360, a humanitarian outreach for peace and empowerment. But I didn't go out into the world to give hope; I wanted to find it. I wanted to reach out to others to help them find peace and empower them because I hated myself and I didn't want them to become like me. I was the one who needed someone to reach out to help me find hope, feel peace, and be empowered.

She saw this too, as if she could read my mind. I remember her words exactly, "You're trying to save others because you hope someone will come and save you."

It wasn't the first time I heard those words. One of my professors at NYU expressed them slightly differently. I was talking to her about a case in my clinical internship. The case was complicated, and I had put myself in a dangerous situation. My professor asked me, "Why did you put yourself in that dangerous situation?"

I replied, "I had to. She was a little girl who was being sexually abused."

My professor, Dr. Flynn, said, "No. You didn't have to. You think you did it for her, but you did it for yourself, because when you were a little girl, nobody came to save you." More than a decade later, I was still saving others as a cry for someone to save me.

I clenched my fist. I was trying not to cry, but I couldn't stop myself. "If you need to cry, cry!" she said with such authority that she startled me.

"I don't want to cry; I'm tired of crying."

"But every time you stop yourself from crying, you keep holding onto your pain. You need to release it."

I wasn't sure if it was her relentless insistence that I face my truth, the care with which she did it, or my exhaustion from maintaining my façade, but I admitted it finally. She was right; I was in pain, and finally I had the courage to say it out loud. That was my first act of true courage.

Although I was inundated with emotions, I listened to every word she said. Something caught my attention, so I asked, "What do you mean I need to release it?"

She pondered for a while and then said, "When you feel these memories coming up and you start to feel the pain, don't stop it; feel it and then let it go." I tried to wrap my head around it, but I had more questions, and she had the right answers.

"What do you mean, 'feel it'? Am I supposed to just allow myself to be in pain? How does it work?"

"You'll know when you're ready," she said.

"But I'm ready now. Tell me what to do, and I'll do it."

"When you're ready, you won't have so many questions. This is not my process; it's yours. I can't tell you what to do. You need to go within."

A force of nature indeed: I wanted a blueprint, but she wouldn't give me one. Instead, she pushed me to go within. Her last words on the matter were, "Don't forget to love yourself."

I felt like I was in for a ride, facing pain I had been running from my entire life, and I had no idea how to love myself. I had hated myself for so long. After years of loathing my shame, I started loathing myself. Hating my shame meant remembering. Hating me—well, that helped me carry on.

Not long after our conversation, I became ill. The first few days, I got up from bed, got ready, and went to work as usual, but the team I worked with was a true reflection of its leader. I remember being in the office and becoming sicker as the day went on. The staff refused to let me stay and took me back to my room. When they dropped me off, they said, "You aren't coming back to the office until you feel better." The days passed, and they came by every day to bring me medicine, food, and water until they had nursed me back to health. However, while I was recuperating, something unexpected happened.

I was staying in a room with barely enough space for a bed. There were no windows and no internet access—only me. I was in a room where I couldn't even see the light of day. My body was weak, and all I could do was lie in bed hoping for a quick recovery. However, that wasn't happening as quickly as I hoped. The illness was taking its course, and the more I fought, the harder it became to manage.

I couldn't get up, and any attempt to leave my bed was followed by another strong episode of illness. I lay there in the dark and began to feel depressed. My mind wandered to thoughts of my journey there. I felt frustrated and thought to myself that I hadn't travelled so far just to end up bedridden. Still, those days reminded me of a similar time in the past, and I thought about my last months at work back home.

Work was going well, or so I thought. I had been stressed, but I didn't mind the stress because it kept me busy—very busy. Busy was good, as it kept my mind off the heartbreak of my shattered personal life. I was so in love, but again, with a love that hurt. It also prevented me from all my self-destructive behaviors. I had become a pro at numbing my pain. Work was just another tool. However, I became so ill that I had to take a medical leave. For a long time, the doctors couldn't figure out what was wrong with me. I had developed a debilitating abdominal pain that barely allowed me to walk, and I began to bleed internally. Months after I had tests, took various medicines, saw countless doctors, and endured surgeries, I visited one more doctor. He was young, and I thought he was inexperienced, but he asked me questions about myself that no other doctor had asked. I couldn't tell if I was in a doctor's office or a psychologist's. After a long series of questions, he asked, "Have you considered that maybe this is a result of stress?"

My immediate reaction was to laugh. Stress was my middle name. But I refused to think that was the cause.

I replied jokingly, "If it was, I'd be dead." He didn't laugh; his face was serious, and I knew I wouldn't like what he was about to say next.

He looked at me and said, "Your condition is life-threatening." My laughter died quickly. We talked about treatment and next steps, but he suggested changing my lifestyle.

I left the office feeling that my body had betrayed me, and I was angry that it was giving up on me. I didn't consider why; I just hated myself more because my body had grown weak. I had refused to deal with my pain for so long that eventually it began to attack me physically. I had no choice but to make some drastic decisions. I made some health-conscious choices to help me heal, and I began therapy. My health started to improve, and soon after, I began to miss my counseling sessions. I felt physically strong again and didn't fear the worse, so I saw no need to keep traveling down memory lane. During the last session, she confronted me gently about the things I revealed and suggested strongly that I work through them. However, I'd had enough, and soon after, I decided to leave it all behind.

Yet here I was, betrayed by my body once again, unable to continue my work, and once again forced to face the memories that raced toward me each time I couldn't find an outlet to escape them. I hated the silence and the darkness. I couldn't fight the voices and the images that came to torment me. Even sleep became my enemy, but insomnia turned out to be the cure for my nightmares.

However, this time it was different. I hadn't come all this way to be ill once again, but I also hadn't come all this way not to find the peace I yearned for so greatly. I remembered what my friend said, "When you feel these memories coming up and you start to feel the pain, don't stop it; feel it and then let it go." She was right; when I was ready, I would know, and in that moment, I was ready.

Although I couldn't see the light of day, it didn't matter, because I felt my light escaping me, and I was desperate to hold on to it. I literally was locked away from the world, away from every possible escape. It was time; I could either feel the pain and release it, or I could continue to allow it to break me down.

My light had been covered by the dark memories of my past for long enough. I had no choice; if I wanted to heal and experience new life, I had to feel the pain and release it once and for all. I yearned for a life in which I wasn't held captive in the shadows of my true self. I had to expose my pain. Yet nothing can prepare you to feel your pain. All you hold on to is the burning will of your heart, because once you choose to take control of your life, it empowers you to face whatever has been holding you back.

The floodgates of tears suddenly sprung wide open. I could feel the forceful surge of my fire within blazing down my walls. The force was unapologetic; it had no reservations, and it was not going to stop. I could feel in my stomach the pain of old wounds resurfacing. Memories came rushing back like flotsam from a shipwreck.

I couldn't control its might. It was powered by the wrath of years of pain buried in my depths, sealed by a door of denial that I finally had chosen to open. I was overtaken by the tormenting affliction that came gushing out of my open wounds. I had torn off the bandage, and I could finally see what was underneath: the unhealed scars from the lashes of pain coated in a bile that sickened my essence and oozed venom that was eating away at me. The pain of every disgusting touch, every hurtful word, and every brutal strike was rising to the surface.

The voices I could never silence suddenly became louder.

"You're nothing."

"You're worthless."

"You will always be a nobody."

"No one will love you—look at you, you're a piece of shit."

"You're garbage. You're a piece of garbage that I picked up from the side of the street."

I cried in agony, but the voices only became louder, and the memories kept surfacing.

"Leave before I stab you. I hope when you walk out that door, a truck runs over you and kills you."

I remembered becoming numb again. I was trying to understand why so much that was vile was spoken into my being. I couldn't understand why anyone who loved me could speak these words to me or wish my death with so much revulsion. However, in that moment, the image of my life being snuffed out by a truck didn't seem as scary as enduring the pain that I was releasing from my emotional body.

I replayed every word and every image in my mind countless times. It was horrifying. The memories crushed me. I kept thinking back to the idea of being crushed by a truck. I started to reason with the idea, to find something merciful in that kind of death. I wondered, was it easy? Would I be killed instantly? Would it be painful? I began to think that my life must be worthless if anyone could wish that for me. Then I started to think that if the people who were supposed to love me could feel that way about me, then maybe everyone felt that way. I was spiraling, regressing. I was only twelve years old when I first adopted those beliefs. At that young and tender age, I was convinced that if the people who are supposed to love me don't, then no one ever will love me. And at twelve years old, I started chasing death.

As difficult as it was, I stayed the course. My memories went back as far as the first of my life and were as recent as my latest heartbreak. However, the memories that resurfaced were the ones that broke away a piece of me and dismembered my soul to such a degree that they dimmed the light in me and trapped me in an abyss of darkness. The more the memories surfaced, the greater the pain. I cried uncontrollably, but I wasn't running from the pain; I wasn't numbing myself; I was experiencing it. I let each memory play itself out in every heartbreaking detail until I became exhausted and fell asleep. Nonetheless, when I awoke, they were waiting there for me again, and again I refused to escape them.

Lying on the bed, unable to move, the physical and emotional exhaustion triggered more memories, and the old narrative began. "This is what you like, right? Come, let me show you what you like. When you grow up, you're going to love this." I started to feel a familiar sensation I hadn't experienced since childhood.

At this point, the narrative of my past was playing itself out, and it seemed that I had no control over it—but I did. My heart was ready, my will surrendered to the pain, and I released it.

The memories kept replaying in my head. I reflected to when I was gang raped as a teenager. I remembered waking up dazed and confused. Before I regained my senses, I could feel them. I remember looking around and seeing one, then another, and another. I began to struggle and heard one grunt, "What are you doing?" Still, I kept struggling until a forceful blow knocked me into a deep sleep.

I remembered another time, staring at a knife to my throat and hearing the words "Shut up or I'll kill you" whispered in my ear, right before he raped me. That time, I wasn't afraid. By then, I knew you can't kill what is already dead.

I felt a sudden painful flare in my stomach. I got up, rushed into the bathroom, and vomited profusely. However, it wasn't my illness; it was my disgust and my shame, the reminder of the hate I felt for myself. I began to feel myself becoming numb again. I was gathering my strength to rebuild the walls. However, I was exhausted mentally and drained emotionally. It had been days—days full of memories of words that were lethal to my mind, blows that were hurtful to my body and slayed my innocence. Yet I remembered something I had forgotten until that point: "Remember to love yourself."

I was back in my bed. Time passed, and I couldn't tell if it was day or night. It seemed like one endless moment in time with so many memories being purged, so many emotions exploding, my defenses imploding, and excruciating pain at the center of it all.

I was feeling the pain, but it wasn't like any I had felt before. It was different. I didn't feel anguish. Every time I felt my pain triggered, I fought it with every ounce of my strength. It took everything in me to numb myself and disconnect until I could finally move on from it without ever truly experiencing the pain, but the process itself was agonizing. My greatest fear about pain was that it would break me, but never releasing my hold on it was doing precisely what I feared the most; it was tearing me apart. I was creating more pain each time I refused to release it; but this time, it was making me whole again.

I was exhausted. I had cried for days. The only time I was free from the familiarity of my days was the time each day my new friends came by with a care package. The gesture was kind, sweet, and thoughtful, but it made me feel uncomfortable. I couldn't understand why they went to such great lengths to take care of me. I felt like I was a nuisance. Then I would beat myself up for not being stronger and having to bother these kind souls. I wrote a message to my dear friend to thank her and apologize for all the inconvenience I was causing everyone. Her reply brought me back to a thought I had earlier. She wrote, "When you learn to love yourself, you will learn to accept love from others. You are no bother at all. You are family, and we love you." As I read her message, my friend's words thundered loudly in my head once again: "Remember to love yourself."

I didn't think I had any tears left, but I did. This time it wasn't surfacing memories that made me cry; it was the realization that I didn't know how to love myself. Even in that moment, I couldn't find a shred of love for myself. All I could think about were all the ways I hated myself: I hated myself for being weak; I loathed my body because I could not bear the disgust; I hated my shame because I couldn't change my past, and I hated the pain that had overpowered me.

From the earliest moment of my victimization, I was tormented by asking myself, "Why me?" I wanted to understand why I had been a victim of so many horrendous acts, what it was about me that made people do terrible things to me. I was too young when I began to question these things and realized that the moment I began to ask such questions, I took the blame away from them and put it on myself.

At first, I believed what I was told as a little girl, that I was a "bad girl" and that I "deserved to be punished." It was easy to believe the lies spewed at me time and time again. According to the people around me, I was, "stupid," "dumb," and "clumsy." I also was "ugly," and I was told things like, "You look like a beast," "Next to a pretty girl, you're ugly," and "No one will ever want you because you'll disgust them." Because I was bombarded constantly with words that humiliated me, I naturally began to think that maybe if I was pretty enough, smart enough, or good enough, people would stop doing bad things to me and I wouldn't be punished as much. Yet the abuse continued, and the unfortunate events in my life exacerbated my self-loathing. I felt like I was never good enough. I was convinced that I wasn't worthy of being loved.

I didn't learn to love myself unconditionally immediately, but for the first time, I grieved for the love I couldn't feel for myself and the affliction of blame that shame imposed on me. I realized that I'd been punishing myself with self-hatred. Others' lies became my own, but I was ready to release those lies that concealed my truth. In that moment, I began to feel a heaviness being lifted, my pain being released.

I remember lying in my bed in silence for a long time, pondering everything that had taken place in the days that led up to that moment. I was neither trying to make sense of anything nor feeling pain. I was simply being. I remained still for a long time, and then I fell into a deep sleep. When I awoke, I began to think about everything again, but this time it was different.

I felt a sense of peace. I was of sound mind, my heart felt courageous, and my spirit felt emancipated. I felt charged with new life, but my process wasn't yet complete. I had made a choice to face my pain, and so I did. For days, I allowed it to surface, and as it did, I felt it all, like a fire burning through my soul. I felt it seize my mind and dredge up every dreadful memory that replayed the horrific scenes of my past. I felt my anger, resentment, guilt, and judgment. I felt my lack of forgiveness and my self-blame. I felt my mortification, embarrassment, and disgust. I felt my shame and hate for everything I saw in myself. But that unremitting self-hatred was now gone. Truth is the beginning of a harmonious alignment between mind, body, and spirit—the genesis of living authentically.

The process was just beginning. I decided to revisit my memories one more time, but this time, I wouldn't look through the veil of deception. My truth dismantled my lies, and that truth was a force with which to be reckoned. I was no longer afraid of the fire; I was the fire. I was resolute in my truth; the blame for my victimization was not mine to bear, and my self-hatred was undone the moment I realized my truth. With a new understanding of who I was, I took a bold step back to the beginning.

I searched deep for any recollection of my earliest memories. I wondered if they all were inundated with abuse, but they weren't. I recalled memories of a playful little girl who liked to laugh. She was a visionary even then. Her imagination took her to worlds that had not yet been discovered. She shared tales with her dolls and believed them to be true. The memories made me smile, but I couldn't help feeling the sadness I saw in her eyes. The memories were mainly of her in isolation, too young to understand, but she knew something made her different. She held secrets that troubled her young mind, but her fear wouldn't allow her to reveal them. The image of her playing began to fade, and an image of a path that led to a sealed door began to emerge. Slowly, I allowed myself to step toward the door until finally I opened it. For the first time, I would allow myself to see behind the sealed door. Unlike other times, I wasn't there to allow him to victimize me again; I was there for her. I watched her face as her toddler's body was ravished. I no longer blamed her. I felt the fear she felt. I felt the hurt she felt. I felt the confusion she felt. And finally, I mourned her innocence. I sobbed uncontrollably, overwhelmed by sadness, and I cried out, "I'm sorry." They were the only words I could muster. I had to ask for her forgiveness. I had blamed her for so long; I had abandoned the memory of her innocence, the tenderness of her spirit, and the bravery of her heart. Because no matter what, she had survived; alone in that nightmare, she had pushed through. The strength of her spirit had not given up on her. The more I remembered my innocence, the more I released the pain of self-blame. All the self-hatred I had carried for blaming my young innocence dissolved finally, and it was no longer my burden to bear.

I continued to recall the memories that stole my innocence, every ruthless strike that marked my soul and every vicious word that crippled my authentic self. In each memory, I rewrote my story. I renounced the life I built on lies, shame, and pain, and I renounced the life I was never meant to live. Then I honored the unadulterated authenticity in my innocence; I venerated the strength of my body to rise and carry on after it had been overcome by force. I released the false self and reclaimed my destiny.

As I began to recover from my open wounds, I also began to recover my health. My thoughts were full of hope, and my heart was full of courage. I was ready to truly begin my journey. I couldn't believe all that had taken place. The heart revealed my pain, and spirit uprooted all that was untrue from my core, guided me into my heart, flooded my wounds with love, and transformed my pain into power. It was my genesis, the first chapter of the story of my authentic self.

Reflection II: Understanding Pain

It was 1989, and I was living in the emerald plush mountains of Puerto Rico, overlooking the infinite beauty of the Caribbean Sea that adorned my Isla del Encanto, La Perla del Caribe. I sat on the porch of our tin-roofed wooden house with my little brother, my mom, and my grandmother, watching the roaring sea rise and listening to the raging winds that announced Hurricane Hugo. The sun was hidden behind the dark clouds, but the power had gone out, and we could still feel it burning through the atmosphere.

We sat in silence for a while, but fear was imprinted on the faces of my little brother and me, who had never experienced the force of nature that was coming upon us. Then, the silence was broken as my grandmother spoke to us. She looked out at the mountains and asked us, "In this storm, would you rather be that tree?" She pointed to a tall tree that stood at the foot of the mountain, one with a trunk so wide it looked like its footstool. Her pointing finger then glided over to the right. "Or would you rather be that?" And her finger pointed to the view of a field of tall grass that marked the path to the mountaintop.

The answer seemed so obvious, and my eleven-year-old mind couldn't see past the obvious, but I still questioned it. Why would I choose to be a fragile stem that looked so insignificant compared to the greatness of this tree that appeared suddenly to be even more powerful in the face of the storm? However, for some odd reason, I couldn't answer the question. Then I heard the sweet, innocent voice of my baby brother exclaim enthusiastically, "The tree!" I watched my mother smile in silence, as if she was remembering this story from when my grandmother told it before, maybe during another storm, or maybe when she was a child like we were.

There was more to the story, and I sat in silence, staring at my grandmother steadily and waiting for her to continue, but she didn't. She wanted me to answer, and so I did. I said what I thought I should say, "I'd be the tree because I want to be strong, Abuelita." I was almost proud. I thought that's what she wanted to hear, that I wanted to be strong.

However, as soon as I answered, I knew that's not what she wanted to hear, and she went on to say, "You see that tree? When the storm comes and the winds grow stronger, its stubbornness and unwillingness to bend with the wind will cause it to break, but they"—she raised her finger again to point to the path to the mountaintop seemingly bejeweled by the field of tall grass—"they won't refuse to bend with the wind because that's their nature, and they will survive the storm. Sometimes we need to know when to bend to the winds of the storm. Don't base your belief in strength on outward appearances. A tree is strong because it gives life. Even if it breaks, its roots can bring forth more life, and it can grow again because that is its nature, but it will suffer. It doesn't always require physical strength to survive a storm; sometimes it requires us to allow nature to take its course, which is a different kind of strength. Now, which one would you rather be?"

When we face the storms of pain, they can either bring out the false beliefs rooted in us or uproot the farce and bring out the strength of our true natures. Yet how do we understand something that can be as deep as the sea, as strong as the wind, and scorching like the sun? You don't stand to understand it; you plant yourself in the grounds of your truth and take root in your true nature. Let the turbulent waters bind you to your truth, the raging winds strengthen your true character, and the power of the burning sun bring light to your truth.

When we are unwilling to remain in our nature in the face of pain, and we rely on our brain mind rather than our heart mind to try to understand it, the strength of our own obstinacy will allow the pain to break us because it goes against the nature of who we were created to be. Finding certainty and being grounded in ourselves allows us to face pain and be willing to experience it without fear that it will change our true nature. Pain is meant to take its course. It is not meant to be understood or denied, because it does not and cannot define us.

Reflection III: Pain in the Familiar

There are only two ways to deal with mental and emotional pain: going without or going within. Mental and emotional pain are caused by external experiences that affect our internal belief system by influencing the way we think and feel about ourselves. This kind of pain can be caused by physical or psychological abuse and neglect, all of which may result in trauma.

Physical abuse is any threat that violates our physical well-being. Moreover, the definitions of psychological, verbal, and emotional abuse and neglect often cross over. Putting it in lay terms, they can be understood as negative verbal statements and (or) emotional treatment that demeans, humiliates, or demoralizes us while violating our sense of dignity and security.

In my experience, abuse produces two types of pain: mental and emotional. Although the two seem connected and often overlap, I didn't always experience them inclusively. They became distinct kinds of pain with their own identities. There were times when I was in mental anguish but didn't feel emotional pain, and there were times when I was in emotional anguish but didn't feel mental pain. Sometimes I was in both mental and emotional agony. However, for the most part, I had developed a coping mechanism to help me numb one or the other, and sometimes both. Numbing was part of my comfort zone, and denial safeguarded me in my comfort by any means of escape.

The false self will lead you to find comfort in external experiences.

For me, it was rapid cycles of chaotic relationships that I knew were doomed to end, self-destructive behaviors that gave me temporary solace, workaholic cycles during which I got no sleep, achieving impossible projects with unrealistic deadlines, taking on worthy causes but building hopeless ideals … all while I abused my health, became sick, recovered, and then did it all over again—anything that helped me escape from me. I was like a lab rat stuck in my cage of denial, stepping onto the running wheel to nowhere whenever I needed to escape.

Familiarity is our comfort, and the false self needs our external experiences, so when in pain, it retreats instinctively to its familiar place and seeks comfort without. The false self finds comfort in superficial validation, false recognition, and hollow support. It will chase a love that hurts. It looks externally for what mirrors it internally, so when we run from internal pain, we will be sure to run right into it. Yet the irony of comfort zones is that eventually they become the place of our greatest discomfort and give us no choice but to seek within if we truly desire to release the pain of our past.

Reflection IV: The False Comfort of Pain

Mental and emotional pain differ from physical pain. Physical pain hurts the point of contact. When a part of our body is injured, we do not question the function or reason for the existence of that body part. Take a wound to the leg, for example; a leg doesn't stop being a leg because it has been wounded. If wounded beyond recovery, no one says, "The leg wasn't a leg," or "The leg should've been an arm instead because it's unsalvageable." Its authenticity and purpose are not questioned or altered because of the injury or the outcome. Even the example seems ludicrous, because it would never happen. However, mental and emotional pain are pervasive and are experienced in every fiber of our beings. These kinds of pain have devastating effects that cause us to question our very essence.

When our lives are affected by mental and emotional pain, our brain mind stores the despair as it stores all information. Our brain processes it as it processes all new information, by relating it and creating connections to the knowledge we have of ourselves and our past experiences. Our brain mind will look for similarities to understand it, and find patterns and make connections to explain it, thereby causing an internal crisis. This happens because mental and emotional pain cause our thoughts and our emotions to become our enemies by causing our brain mind and our heart mind to be at odds with one another, because while our brain mind is storing information indiscriminately and revising our knowledge and our sense of self with each new experience, our heart mind is rejecting indiscriminately that which doesn't belong to the authentic self.

However, mental and emotional pain are not meant to be understood or explained. They're meant to be felt so that we can tend to them with love and care, so that the wounds they cause can heal. They are not intended to prompt us into action and seek without; they are meant to halt our actions and take us deep within ourselves to remember our truth.

Our truth is the only remedy for the pain, but when we are not aligned with our authentic selves, the very thought of confronting the pain is daunting, and the process appears even more excruciating. Our false self is only a construction of external experiences, and without them, the construction will come tumbling down easily.

Our immediate instinct to want to soothe the pain so we don't feel it, triggers the internal crisis, and therefore, those instincts revert to the familiar. If your sense of self has become intricately dependent on your external experiences, it will try to soothe it by going without. However, there is no medicine that can numb such pain. The only remedy is to feel it and soothe it with our truth. We must acknowledge pain and feel it so we can then release it through the power of our truth. Preventing the pain from doing what it is intended to do—protect us by making us aware of hurtful distortions to our truth—doesn't allow us to heal and release the pain from our mental and emotional bodies.

When we are faced with something that threatens our core, we need to go within, but the very idea of going there—where the pain lives—paralyzes us and arouses our fear. Fear is the paralysis caused by the pain that is dictating our life. Trying to understand and explain it engenders confusion, doubts, and insecurities that become embodied in fear. Pain and fear activate our survival instincts, which revert to finding comfort in the familiar the moment we are faced with the need for freedom from pain. Thus, it us up to us to challenge ourselves to wash out the fear and go within.

Reflection V: The Cry of My Pain

For a time, pain was all I knew. Pain became my comfort zone. I journeyed through life mostly in the absence of myself, in a world full of contradictions, trapped between who I was created to be and who I was made out to be. I was entangled in a web of confusion, without direction or vision.

I knew only suffering and journeyed in agony. I was trapped in a recurring nightmare that never let me see the light of day. Anger, sadness, and loneliness were my daily bread. Betrayal, pain, and sorrow sustained me. Through my veins, I felt a bloody torrent of rage that continued to pierce through me without breaking the skin and allowed no escape. My anger and bitterness became toxic and ate away to the heart of me. My unhealed wounds left my soul naked and my spirit broken. And all of it led to a one-way street called pain, traveled in a vehicle of shame.

I learned to hide my pain behind a smile and find comfort in my tears. The desperation in my laughter went unnoticed, and the cry in my silence was mistaken for peace. I was a whirlwind of contradictions. My truth had been buried beneath layers of unworthiness, despair, and hopelessness. I kept reliving my pain because my wounds had never healed. I was absorbed in trying to understand my pain, so I kept recreating it. I was consumed by pain so totally that I became it, and every experience became a mirror reflection of who I had become.

When we don't allow pain to take its course, it will dictate our course.

Part IV

The Heart's Burning Flame

Breaking the Illusion of Pain

Once, while visiting my cousin, we talked about my victimization. She asked me casually to do an exercise of sorts. She instructed me to close my eyes, so I did. Then she asked, "What do you see?" At first, I saw nothing, including the point of going along with her request. However, I concentrated a little more, but I felt very anxious. I didn't know what I would see; the mere thought of it scared me, and I didn't know why. A few minutes passed, and I started thinking to myself that I was in a safe place with someone I trusted, and my anxiety lessened. But then, there it was. I saw an image of myself and began to cry. My cousin asked for a second time, "What do you see?"

I replied, "I see me."

I imagine my crying confused her, and she asked again, "Yes, but what do you see? How do you see yourself?"

I was choking on my tears, but finally I said, "I see myself, ravished. There are scars all over my body. My face is disfigured by the scars, and I am unrecognizable, but I know it's me."

A cold chill went down my spine. I could feel the suffering of that image in my bones. It was the first real insight I had into my self-worth and my suffering. I didn't believe I was worthy of more. To me, I was nothing more than a worthless victim. Despite my success, the accolades, and my large social network, I didn't see myself the way the world seemed to see me. I was deceived by the illusion of pain.

While we remain trapped in that illusion, the real pain stays trapped in our emotional bodies, changing the narrative of our lives until we choose to reclaim our power. The power that we hold is our free will, the power of choice.

We have the power to choose to face our pain and release it from our emotional bodies. We can choose to let the fire in our souls consume the pain and release it so that we can venture beyond and into our authentic selves.

Fourth Insight

Power is the discovery of the authentic self.

Be willing to be the most powerful expression of your authentic self.

A Burning Heart Ignites Power

We are the protagonists in the stories of our lives. But when we are victimized, sometimes we absorb the pain, trapping it within, changing the nature of its course and transforming it into venom that, in turn, changes the narrative of our stories.

The word *victim* refers to any person who has experienced an event likely to cause pain. It does not apply to a specific individual who has suffered any one form or degree of victimization but to all who have endured a painful, life-changing event.

The pain endured during victimization also varies from one experience to another, and the way in which the victim deals with the pain varies as well. However, there is a presumed commonality among victims; unknowingly, many form an attachment to the pain and assume a victim identity. Thus, post-victimization, the person holds on to the pain, and it permeates throughout that person's being and changes the individual's character by adopting an identity defined by the victimization, the victim identity.

The victim identity is one of the most pronounced personas of the false self, because pain has a direct effect on our core being. Our core is the gateway to our authentic self and serves as the conduit that brings forth the pure essence of our existence.

When our core is threatened, it will seek to guard itself so that pain cannot penetrate it, but in the meantime, it also wards off the powerful expression of our authenticity.

The victim identity only keeps life entangled in pain. In my case, it allowed me to remain in a place of hurt where I felt nothing but despair, grief, and hopelessness. Unknowingly, my suffering became its own gateway to resentment, bitterness, and lack of forgiveness. I was in pain, and I needed the world to know it. The emotions affirmed my pain. I felt validated by my victim identity. However, the deeper I went within, the more I discovered that idle emotions—those that enable our resistance to go deep within to the root cause of our pain—were only the illusion of pain.

Idle emotions keep us in a recurring state of suffering that deceives the mind into believing that we are dealing with the pain of our victimization. The word *suffer* means to endure pain. The moment the pain is inflicted, we suffer. But thereafter, the suffering we attribute to our victimization is merely a fabrication of the real pain our emotions create; it is not the real pain. The suffering serves as a defense mechanism because the emotions prevent the real pain from surfacing and allowing us to release it. Eventually, however, the armor begins to eat away at our soul, because the real pain is still within and was never meant to be part of the fabric of our being.

I thought my pain was so great that I would never know life without it. I couldn't even begin to fathom such a life. Pain resonated with me; I identified with it, and it defined me. I felt comfortable in it to such an extent that I found comfort in it. Pain was part of who I was, embodied in my false self. I felt like a casualty of life, and I was. But I was a casualty of life by choice. It was I who continued to revictimize myself. Every day that I chose to hold on to the victim identity, I also chose to hold on to the pain. By remaining in my victimhood, I relived the horrific memories of my victimization constantly and allowed them to demoralize me until they shamed me and tormented me until I broke. My offenders were no longer holding me down, defiling my body, striking me senseless, or speaking cruelly into my ears, but every day, I chose to remain a victim and relinquished my power. I was surrendering my authentic self to the false self. I did so until I felt drained of my essence. The emptiness overpowered me, and the life pulse of my hollow heart made me feel worthless.

Unworthiness is a self-inflicted judgment that ensues from internalizing our victimization and attributing the blame to ourselves. I call this the victim-perpetrator syndrome, which occurs when we assume both roles in the victimization. We assume the hurt inflicted in the role of the victim, but we also assume the burden of culpability of inflicting the hurt, the role of the perpetrator. Self-blame occurs as a direct result of the maladaptive beliefs associated with the victimization.

The danger lies in the trap of self-blame. When we blame ourselves for the hurt we suffer, we also believe that we deserve that hurt as a form of punishment. As a result, we trap ourselves in an endless cycle of revictimization through self-punishment. In the meantime, self-blame brews guilt, guilt brings forth shame, and ultimately, we have the perfect recipe for unworthiness.

Guilt is the feeling of carrying the burden of responsibility. Shame is the agonizing feeling of humiliation associated with the victimization, so when we blame ourselves, it makes us feel worthless because we also feel the guilt and shame of the perpetrator. It's not the pain of the victimization that makes us feel worthless; it's the self-blame that makes us afraid to face ourselves and go deep within. Yet unworthiness can hold power over us only until the moment we decide to break free from the bonds of victimhood, simply by choosing to know that we are worthy of more.

Our lives reflect the choices we make. My life certainly became a reflection of my choice to play the victim in the story of my life. The familiar state of suffering became my safeguard from having to deal with the pain I experienced. For many years, I felt like I was drowning in my pain. But I wasn't; I was drowning in my emotions. However, pain is not an emotion; it is a level of consciousness that we experience in our emotional body. Pain is the safeguard against our authentic selves. Pain absorbs every negative experience and embodies every harmful act, and we hold the power to release it. We have the power to choose the narrative of our lives. In our hearts burns the will to release our divinity and be the authentic self.

The Journey with Power

Reflection I: The Annihilator of Narratives

When victimization disrupts the narrative of our stories, everything we know becomes nothing as we've known it.

Our humanity is expressed fully in our brain mind, while our spiritual being—the source of our authenticity—is expressed fully in our heart mind. However, victimization eradicates our reliance on our heart mind and leads us to rely instead solely on the brain mind, thereby distorting the natural course of the powerful expression of our authentic self and annihilating the true narratives of our lives.

Many of us can't remember the shift, the time when we forsook our authentic self for the false self, perhaps because our painful experience occurred early in childhood or was too traumatic or subtle. In any case, the shift begins to narrate its own story.

The heavy dependence on our brain mind that we develop over time blocks us from the guidance of our heart mind and causes internal disharmony. The disharmony is the root cause of experiencing the self through our affliction and not in the perfection, wholeness, and completeness in which we were created.

When the shift occurs, we feel defeated rather than victorious, doubtful rather than confident, hopeless rather than hopeful, weak rather than strong, fearful rather than courageous. These attributes of our spirit become fleeting emotions that we chase through external validations because the false self does not possess the attributes of our authentic self. We become ensnared in their absence, unaware that even the very desire for these attributes is an admission that we do not possess them. However, this simply is the memory of the victimization living through us again in our daily experience and crippling our self-worth.

Victimization is not a matter of choice. We don't choose to be victimized; victimization is forced upon us. When we are violated by someone else's false reality of the self, it rapes our will, and the imprint of the victimization leaves us wounded.

Victimization does not discriminate. It can affect us physically, emotionally, or mentally. It can appear in many forms. Some forms seem more tolerable than others, while some leave deeper wounds. Some leave visible scars, while others only can be felt. It has unlimited sources—it can be perpetrated by an individual, such as a stranger or even a loved one. Alternatively, it can also come from the universal, such as a community or a natural catastrophe. The source is irrelevant; the root of our illusory pain lies in the imprint that it leaves behind.

The imprint of an event stored in our memory is responsible for the events that replay in our brain minds long after the events have passed. For the most part, there are two types of memories we tend to recall most: those associated with great joy and those associated with great pain.

Our lives tend to be defined by the thoughts, feelings, emotions, and ideas associated with our memories. Thus, positive memories tend to generate thoughts of inspiration, feelings of pleasure, and emotions of happiness. Conversely, if memories of great pain outweigh those of great pleasure, our lives tend to align with thoughts of disillusionment, feelings of despair, emotions of grief, and ideas of hopelessness. Memories of being victimized can feel like the heaviest of all painful burdens to which we attach ourselves. We can reduce that burden only when we learn to let go and go beyond.

To let go of the victim and go beyond, we must go within, into our heart mind. Only with our heart mind can we defy logic and reason, know that we are not defined by our experiences, and release any attachment of our thoughts, feelings, emotions, and ideas to the victimization.

Reflection II: Seared in Self-Blame and Rising Again

Victimization makes us feel powerless. The illusion of pain causes delusions of identity once the malevolence of self-blame seeps into your core and is manifested as shame.

I felt shamed by my victimization, and my shame led to the unworthiness that kept me bound to my victim identity. For me, surviving meant remaining immobile on innumerable occasions and enduring the gruesome act of violation. I was just a scared little girl trying to survive. But those moments haunted me for a great part of my life. I blamed myself, and I went on to believe those moments defined me. Yet I was allowing the pain inflicted in those moments to define me—and not the strength that carried me through those stormy epochs.

My survival required true grit to withstand the pain and persevere through the anguish of my self-blame. The fiber of my being defied all logic; my heart pulsated with the strength of my spirit and spoke the language of my soul. Still, my shame wouldn't allow me to feel past the guilt that ate away at me, so I could own my strength, the strength that fueled my faith, inspired my hope, and powered my courage during my darkest nightmares. Self-blame will obscure everything that matters, but we must shatter the illusion of pain so that we can see our worth.

This is the thing about victimization. It happens in the physical realm, but it tries to penetrate our spirit. However, unless we give it our power, it is powerless.

We can be victimized physically, mentally, and emotionally, but our essence is unchangeable. What changes is the uninhibited expression of our authentic selves. However, we have the power of choice. We are the power of our authenticity.

When our well-being feels threatened, our basic human instincts mobilize to ensure our survival. However, those instincts are connected to our brain mind, which only ensures survival through logic, reason, and understanding. Our heart mind helps us not only survive but also overcome and go beyond the experience, because the strength of our spirit abides in the assurance of knowing the true self. Our authentic self is resolute in perfection and wholeness and cannot be defined by experiences or circumstances. We are not our story; we are the power of the narrative, and we have the power to choose that narrative.

In a time of crisis, our instinctive thoughts don't reason or make compromises with a threat, and they don't make choices based on logic—instead, they help us survive. Many of us become stuck in that narrative. We tend to judge ourselves accordingly, viewing ourselves as compromised and lacking reason and judgment because we couldn't prevent the story from unfolding. Nonetheless, a chapter in our lives does not tell the full story. The full narrative is unwritten; we can make the choice to live today the story we want to tell tomorrow.

The illusion of pain caused the delusion of my victim identity. I had to make a choice to shatter the illusion and purge myself from the malevolence of self-blame that had me ensnared in vile shame.

I identified myself with the victim and judged myself accordingly. I know now that my choice required me to summon my heart to access every ounce of strength in my spirit to endure the unthinkable. I was present in the horrific acts of someone else's story, but they had no power to change the nature of my being.

Our strength is in the power of knowing that our authentic self is impenetrable and immutable, and we can choose to be the most powerful expression of our authentic self. The spirit that helps us endure does not leave us trapped in our victimization. It is the force of nature that wills us to endure, survive, and overcome so that we can rise again.

The moment we choose to face our demons, we affirm our worth. We rise and confront the eye of the storm that has been swirling inside, only to learn that we are the true force of nature with which to be reckoned.

Reflection III: Reclaiming Our Power

The choices we make about the beliefs in our self-worth, after we have suffered immeasurably in the face of the unimaginable, determine our destiny. What we are willing to believe about our self-worth has a direct effect on the way in which we manifest our lives. When we believe that we deserve to suffer, we will continue to attract pain. Conversely, when we believe we are worthy, we will settle for nothing less than that which reflects our worthiness. In life, we manifest the value we place on our self-worth.

When we endure great challenges, it is easy to lose our sense of self-worth. When we lose that, our sense of purpose lives in the shadows of unworthiness, our destiny is trapped in shame, and our authentic self becomes buried beneath the layers of our false self.

We must reclaim our power. We must choose to change our thinking to eliminate negative thought patterns that lead to the self-destructive behaviors that keep us stuck in a life of insufferable pain. We must choose to believe we are worthy.

I am aware that these words may sound harsh at first and even unkind. At least that's how I felt the first time I realized that the pain I'd been carrying with me like titanium armor, pulling me each day deeper into my abyss of despair, was a matter of choice. Yes, this was the harshest reality I had to confront. It wasn't the pain but the realization that I was in pain, because it was my choice to hold on to it by denying my worthiness.

I felt enslaved by my pain every day, but every day it was me who made the choice to believe I was worthless. That choice is what kept me suffocating in my pain, unable to fulfill my purpose and live out my destiny. I had to reclaim my power and choose to believe that I was worthy of being perfect, whole, and complete.

Reflection IV: Changing the Narrative

I am too familiar with being at a crossroads, choosing between the familiarity of victimhood or going beyond. It is not an easy impasse to face in our journey, although I learned later that we make it as difficult or as easy as we allow.

At first, trying to break away from my familiar thought and behavior patterns was extremely difficult. I went through so many rapidly recurring stages of self-assurance and then doubts, ups and downs, and great fear—but also great courage. There were days when all I wanted to do was give up, but there also were days when I wanted to shout to the world how glorious it was to discover who I truly am. It was like observing the balancing act between my false self and my authentic self. It became difficult to believe I was on any path at all, much less one of self-actualization, but I was.

Peeling back the layers of my false self and discovering my authentic self wasn't a smooth transition. It was messy, and at times it felt chaotic. I struggled with this feeling. I yearned for nothing more than my version of simplicity and stability. But I had made a choice; I chose to change the narrative of my story.

I became aware fully that I could choose to remain living as my false self, in which I repeated the vicious cycles of my past, reflected the ugliness of its persona, and found temporary relief in false comforts, or I could choose my authentic self, a life in my authenticity, the most powerful expression of my true self.

While I transitioned from living my lie to living my truth, my duality became exposed. Facing my false self made me feel overcome by fear, but I learned that fear is the measure of great courage.

Before I could embrace everything that I am, I had to come to know everything I was not. Every step of the way taught me valuable lessons. Each lesson helped me peel off another layer, and in the absence of it all, I finally met my authentic self and changed the narrative of my story—I was no longer a victim. I was a survivor, one who overcame all the odds against me. I was perfect, whole, and complete.

Reflection V: The Power to Release and Go beyond the Pain

We have many reasons to remain in the familiar. Our defenses justify our reasons for not embarking on the quest for self-actualization. The moment spirit leads our thoughts in the direction of true expression, our defenses are triggered. Spirit knows no limits, and for this reason, it makes no exceptions for pain. No matter how bitter the hurt, spirit only knows vigor and strength. Spirit will always move in the direction of that which our hearts desire and that for which we long.

Conversely, our defenses know only limitations, and their only purpose is to confine us. When pain is all we know, we conform to familiarity. We learn to manage the familiar pain, and in the meantime, we become obsessed with the fear of any further pain, because what we have endured already has devastated us. That fear enables us to create defenses that we believe will protect us from future pain. But fear, unlike spirit, is a primitive human emotion that is flawed, limited, and of no avail. Therefore, that which is a direct result of fear embodies our finite human characteristics, limited in nature, and can only provide the illusion of relief, but no real solution without the guidance of spirit.

We must be aware that we have created defense mechanisms so sophisticated that they are triggered as soon as they feel a threat. It is threatening to be confronted by anything outside the scope of the familiar. When there is a perceived danger, our defenses mobilize and work against any conceivable threat. At times, our defenses appear to have prevented some likely emotional hurt. It is this illusion that perpetuates the cycle of disempowerment. The truth is people cannot cause us emotional suffering unless we give them the power to do so. However, unless we are ready to claim that power, we are likely to live our lives as victims of our circumstances.

Similarly, our defenses also prevent us from allowing the good to enter. Spirit is all good. Its light will seek to permeate our minds and manifest our true potential and purpose by willing the liberation of our authentic self. This is the relentless drive we call hope and is the reason we seek answers. But because we have acceded to the lies of the false self, shifting our thinking to the truth is unfamiliar, and our defenses perceive it as a threat. They will trigger our self-preservation and try to prevent us from shifting to the true expression of the self.

We cannot underestimate the fear of losing our selves. We spend a lifetime building our defenses because we believe they protect us from unwanted emotional pain. Denial allows us to either pretend that everything is okay and continue the same vicious cycle that holds us captive, or if we recognize the vicious cycle, it allows us to justify it by denying there is anything we can do about it.

When our spirit calls us into the heart of our essence, and familiarity loses its sense of purpose, it is not surprising that we feel threatened and our defenses are mobilized without hesitation. It is a critical moment in our lives when spirit moves us away from complacency and toward enlightenment—we can either allow our defenses to seal the door to our true path or embrace it.

Nevertheless, more times than not, when we find ourselves at a crossroads, it is easier to deny that which we don't know than that which we do. Even when we realize that fear is crippling our lives, we deny the fear and justify the crippling, so that we may remain in the familiar. To face the denial requires facing the pain that gave rise to the fear that binds you to your past.

Defenses may seem difficult to overcome, especially when we are not aware when they are operating on our behalf. I have come to learn to detect my defenses when I sense resistance. With this awareness, I have come to understand when spirit is challenging me to go in a new direction or simply deeper within.

We have many opportunities for change in our lifetimes. We will accept the invitation, not when we are ready, as we believe mistakenly, but when we grow tired of stagnation and make the bold choice to move from complacency to greatness. When the flame in our heart begins to dwindle, it steels the pulse that keeps us alive, and our spirits begin to thirst for more; when that insatiable thirst is greater than our need for familiarity, change will occur.

Change comes in great measure. But if we decide to refuse the invitation for a better life, we only prolong the yearning for something greater. In the meantime, all we continue to do is create escapes from our true self. When these escapes happen frequently, they become our reality, because we starve the yearning in our spirits until we numb ourselves to life. We must ask ourselves if our escape has the life, the passion, the love, and the purpose we crave so desperately. Or, do we dare to choose change?

Yes, the sting of our old wounds will paralyze us temporarily but only to provide a way for our suffering to be released. Yes, we are jolted to a halt because our core can be shifted into releasing the pain embedded in the center of our existence by no other means. Our own negation of the pain that is crippling our souls becomes shackled to the pain of the past. Yes, it may seem like a painful process; after all, we have dedicated our lives to creating defenses against the pain, and it has corroded our inner being, preventing us from developing the tools we need to process the pain and release it. But we are worth it.

We must find solace in our hope and trust the process that is moving us to higher levels of consciousness and awareness. The pain of letting go is not a new pain; the pain we feel is the release of the pain we have been holding on to, what we feel is the pain loosening its hold on us.

If we can come to the realization that we are always feeling the pain that we refuse to let go— only disguised differently—we wouldn't be so afraid to face it and deal with the discomfort. Every broken relationship, disenchantment and failure is our pain disguised, which expresses itself in our mental anguish, emotional devastation and physical distress. Our relationships with our families and friends are broken because they reflect the pain we carry inside. Our significant others can never fulfill us because we are broken to begin with. Our jobs weigh heavily on us because we have not discovered our purpose and who we truly are. Our finances are in disarray because we have not discovered our true value, so we wander aimlessly without knowing what we really want. Our zest for life is fueled quickly by fleeting emotions and is extinguished easily by circumstances. The barrenness of pain weighs us down, a dead weight that becomes toxic to our spirits, and the indifference of denial becomes a crutch to help us bear the unbearable.

We have been feeling the pain we have tried to avoid so desperately every day of our lives- knowingly or unknowingly. The events that shaped our very core have been playing themselves out throughout our lives with different characters. Sometimes we have even stumbled upon a path of self-discovery and what we have known all along—the source of our pain. How can we forget the pain that has exhausted our very lives; the mental abuse that resonates in our insecurities; the emotional neglect that left us longing; the lack that sent us off to an unforgiving world; the brutal strikes that have justified our sense of worthlessness; and the loss that birthed our agony? There is no need for self-discovery. We are too aware of the source of our pain, so we hope to discover a different truth, one that will excuse us from dealing with the pain from which we have been running. But we must face it instead.

We remember the pain that changed the course of our lives every day because every day our spirit is telling us that the path we are on is not one that leads us to fulfill our destiny. When we are on the wrong path, we remember that pain every day, in the morning when it appears to steal our sunshine, and at night when it steals our dreams. The devastating effect of our pain makes us want to forget. Every day when we wake up, we hope to forget, but we can't. All our circumstances remind us of the trauma that broke us. Those who ravished us remain like still images in our minds taunting us, and the events that stole our identity replay themselves in the late hours of the night unapologetically. We have been running frantically, hoping never to stand in that place of pain where we once knew ourselves, but can no longer recognize the image of ourselves. We have been blaming ourselves and punishing ourselves ever since the victimization. We deny the fact that any alternate path to our true selves prevents us from releasing the pain, which ultimately leads us to self-destruction. But hope is in truth, and our truth is within.

We are not to blame for the pain that has crippled our lives. But we are responsible for perpetuating it. This is the truth that our spirit comes to reveal. This is the truth that we avoid. This is the truth that appears to be more painful than the source of our pain. But to know our truth is to know our power.

We must recognize that the power in accepting this truth is that we are also accepting the power to change our lives. Every choice we make has a ripple effect on our destiny. The ripple can flow soothingly into the vast of greatness or it can carry the torrents of our past and grow into a gushing tsunami that will devastate our lives to their ends. However, the ultimate truth is that we hold the power to release the pain and go beyond.

Every End Is Only
the Beginning

Part V

Discovering the Authentic Self

Letting Go

We can always remember the hurt that ravished our virgin spirits. In that devastation, time stands still. We stay in the pool of hurt, unable to move forward until the pain cages us in. For me, time pressed on, but my life became stagnant.

While in pain, we can no longer continue our journey vibrant and full of life. The eagerness to live, the readiness to laugh, and the willingness to love are subsumed by pain. Some of us don't remember what it was like to be happy and full of life. Our only reminders are the smiles and laughter of children, the innocence we once knew, long ago.

When something happens that creates so much pain, life as we know it ends and takes a detour. The path on which we begin to journey is built on sorrow. With time, the sorrows are silenced by new challenges that await us unavoidably at every turn, because we were never meant to be on that path. But we press on anyway, trying to create as much distance from that hurtful place as we can, without realizing we are destroying our future. After a while, the life we create in our grief is the only world we really know. And how do we part from the only thing we know for the sake of an unforeseen destiny?

This is probably the most frightening concept for our minds to grasp. No one wants to be a spectator when our own world collapses before our eyes, much less cause the destruction of the fortress we built to protect ourselves. The easiest thing seems to be to remain in the familiar and continue to fuel the vicious cycle that dictates the course of our lives. The most difficult choice we face is the choice to let go.

However, when we are ready to be the most powerful expression of our authentic selves, we need to remember we are mind, body, and spirit. Fulfillment comes when the sum of all parts forms a harmonious whole in the expression of the authentic self. The authentic self is the purest manifestation of the self, and it is perfect, whole, and complete. Our authenticity is our truth, and our truth is our power. My truth is expressed uniquely through me, just as yours is expressed uniquely through you, but it is a truth that can be discovered only by going within. When life presents us with an invitation to go within, with each step we take into our hearts, we peel away the layers that separate us from our greatness, because in the end, the illusory walls of pain from the past are annihilated, and the imaginary fear of the future is shattered. Then, all we have left is the gift of the present, the unadulterated expression of our most powerful being, the authentic self.

Fifth Insight

We alone are the authors of our destinies. Our stories are the
manifestations of that which we chose with fear in the false
self or that which we choose with the bravery of our heart
in the authentic self. To choose is our power to create.

Be willing to live the passion of your spirit that lives in the love in
your heart and be the light of your soul in your authentic self.

The Gift

"You are the gift that you have been waiting for." These are the words of the man who nursed my soul, Donald Bey. They were the compass to my authentic self.

My process did not occur overnight. So much led up to that point: experiences I needed to have, lessons I needed to learn, and wisdom I needed to gain. With each step, my desire to reach my full potential needed to grow, my determination to live out my destiny needed to be strengthened, and my determination to become the most powerful expression of my authentic self needed to be fortified and become irrefutable.

I reclaimed my power when I made the choice to no longer allow shame to keep me bound to the past and allow pain to control my life. I was empowered by my choice and it gave me the strength to revisit the place of my victimization, the memories that haunted me. I had grown tired of being a victim and reliving the hurt inflicted on me. I became tired of living someone else's story. Each day that I lived in my victimization, I was giving away my power, so I broke through the barriers of my shame, acknowledged that I was in pain, and released my burden, a process so powerful that I became power-full. I faced my false self with the truth of my authentic self, let my light overpower my darkness, and rewrote my story.

I had to go in search of my truth within, in order to understand the way in which my past had affected my life, how the lies I believed about myself were not mine to bear, how I played a role in perpetuating the pain by denying the pain rather than releasing the pain, how I was not defined by my past or my experiences, how being my authentic self was not about reaching a destination but who I needed to allow myself to be, and how my power never could be taken, as it has and will always be within me.

We all have choices, and therefore we all have the power to create our destinies. By that, I mean to create the purest manifestation of the most powerful expression of our authentic selves. It is up to us to make that choice, to be fearless, to be limitless.

Every one of us who denies the truest expression of our authentic self also denies the full expression of our greatness. Our uniqueness is our greatness. For this reason, no one can give us the answers, and no one can map out our process. This is a path we must create, a journey that we must undertake individually. We must venture out on our own because the process will take us within, into our hearts, where no one can go but us.

When we have been ensnared by the identity of the false self, we are always looking for ways outside ourselves to fulfill ourselves. However, real fulfillment comes from our authenticity, the freedom to be all we were created to be. The desires in our hearts are the gravitational pull in the direction of our destinies.

Our heart mind reveals our vision and brings forth our divinity—the force that is the unconquerable spirit within us that begins where science ends. It is the inexplicable nature that we find in our faith, hope, and resilience; the inspiration that ignites our imagination, creativity, and innovation; the power that fuels our drive and determination and gives us choice.

The circumstances in our lives can hurt us, but only we can tear ourselves down. We cannot measure ourselves by the adversity that will never equal our divinity. We cannot compare ourselves to illusions the false self creates, because they will be eradicated by our authentic self. We cannot define ourselves by our past, because our future is created by the power we hold in the present. We cannot confine ourselves to darkness, because our light will overpower it.

Our authentic self is our limitlessness. Our unblemished truth has no boundaries. It knows no religion, no race, no gender, no class. It cannot be labeled by our socioeconomic status or our country of origin. It is blind to color, physical impediments, and sexual orientation. It cannot be suppressed by segregation, oppression, or discrimination. It is not limited by space or time, and it is not bound to any human experience. Our authenticity is the perfection of flaws, the strength of weaknesses, and the limitlessness of impossibilities. Our truth is the light that overpowers the darkness. We are the power. We are the gift for which we have been waiting.

May we be limitless and never let anyone else hold the pen that writes our stories, because of seven billion people in this world, there is only one of you—the authentic self.

When you are ready, you will know—and don't forget to love yourself.

Prelude

I woke up frantic. I had another dream, one of many that became my nightly companions. It had been almost two years since I left home. Now I was back home but not quite sure what the word *home* meant anymore. But there I was, home.

When I began to travel two years earlier, I started to have vivid dreams about death and rebirth, the past and the future, pain and wishful desires. Life was happening in my dreams, although some seemed more like nightmares.

Two years later, life still seemed to be happening in my dreams. I was home again with disturbed sleep, and, well, it just all felt too familiar. That's when it hit me: everything had changed, but everything was the same—and vice versa, nothing had changed, and nothing felt the same.

I looked out the window into the dreary sky, trying to find the sunset in the distant view of the New York City skyline, but I couldn't see it. Everything was covered in gray skies and heavy smog. I began to think about my time of rainbow sunrises and golden sunsets on the warm beaches of Thailand. I pictured myself sitting outside the villa that became home in Koh Phangan. I thought about the way it looked out to the vast blue sea that was my daily inspiration. I couldn't help but think that I had finally arrived at the place I sought so desperately in search of my destiny. Everything seemed so clear then.

I had already journeyed to several countries before arriving in Thailand. Each country gifted me with profound experiences that became lessons that changed the course of my life forever. I suddenly felt melancholy and I thought back to my time in Malaysia—Malaysia the Great, that's what I call it. I had been in Malaysia right before arriving in Thailand. It was there that I had my great awakening—or so I thought. It was there that I confronted my demons, there that I faced my pain and reclaimed my power.

My thoughts wondered back to my time in Thailand, I was remembering how it felt to arrive in Thailand after my time in Malaysia. I was overwhelmed by euphoria. I could never forget that feeling. I felt empowered, hopeful, and joyous. Then I started thinking about the fact that I almost didn't make it there. Before my time in Malaysia, I was in Indonesia, that was the beginning of my world tour- my journey within.

In Indonesia I was living and volunteering at an orphanage, an orphanage I had discovered a year before I quit my job as CEO and left home to travel the world. In the most unforeseen twist of events, I woke up on a New Year's Eve day and saw a post on Instagram—it was a picture of the beautiful beaches of Bali—and by four o'clock that afternoon, I was on a flight to Bali. The trip was a catalyst for what was to come. A year later, I was saying goodbye to the life I knew and beginning my journey in Bali.

While I was in Bali, I volunteered at an orphanage that housed children who were victims of extreme poverty, physical and sexual abuse, and child trafficking. I spent my days and nights there. Their lives became my life, until I began to lose track of time. I knew that no matter how long I was there, it would not be long enough. I was overwhelmed by the emotional need and the trauma that weighed heavy on their hearts. I began to contemplate staying long-term and making it my new home.

One night, I had a dream. I was in a maze-like room, and every corner led to a memory in my past that haunted me. In the dream, I began to feel a burning sensation in my skin, and when I looked down at it, I was peeling layers off my skin. The horrifying sight awoke me.

That night, I realized that the greatest weight on my heart was my victimization. Not long after, I was off to Malaysia; it was time. I was ready to face my demons, I was ready to let go.

Back home my mind drifted once again to my time in Thailand- Koh Phangan to be exact. I was dreaming of the little sunny Gecko Villa where I gave birth to *The Woman in the Mirror*- the journey to my authentic self. Now, I'm home- seeing gray skies again, not the clouds of the skyline of a city I have always known as home but of the questions hovering over me, suspended in my polluted thoughts. *I've faced my past and released my pain*—I thought. *I've accomplished great goals and been to the mountaintop. I've met many people and reached destinations in all corners of the earth, and here I am again, surrounded by everything from which I ran.*

Suddenly, I went beyond my thoughts, and in that moment, I realized I had learned a great many things. My awakening was in the realization that neither my past nor my pain defined me, nor was there a goal I needed to accomplish, a mountain I needed to conquer, people I needed to meet, or a destination I needed to reach. My awakening was in knowing that I am nothing and I am everything, that the spirit that abides in me is limitless, and that in knowing my truth, I have come to know my power.

I was resolute in my truth; my destiny is within, and my purpose is to live the most powerful expression of my authentic self. I couldn't help but ponder—*Now that I've stripped off the layers of the false self and now that I know who I am not, who am I? Who is my authentic self? How does she realize herself in the world?*

A sudden surge was brewing within. It was the awakening of a dormant insight, the revelation of my being—I am woman, and that alone had its own meaning of my place in this world. It was the realization that within me lies the inherited genetic makeup of generations of a type of being, a female being, that has nuzzled life in their womb and birthed generations and nations. It was the realization that the demise of my kind, by his kind, was now my rise.

It was the realization that the voices that were forcibly silenced were irreversibly mighty now and roaring within me.

"I Am Woman," I repeated to myself over and over, and I then I started to write in my journal, "to no one will I conform, confusing you all, because to you I am only your lady or your whore, but you can no longer stifle me, instead watch me soar. Depict me at your will, but you won't break my will. Minimize me, but I recognize me, you won't get my apology. I found my voice, to you an intimidating lover, but knowledge is my power." I didn't understand what was happening, but I knew the journey continued.

I was feeling outraged at that moment. My thoughts were drowned out by the continuous news of a category five hurricane that devastated my island, Puerto Rico. The home of my soul had been ravished, and as I looked at the images displayed on the news, all I saw was darkness.

My journey had given me a new sense of boldness and courage. I no longer lingered in wondrous plains of victimization. I was aware of my power. My spiritual consciousness had woken my social consciousness. That which we are in this world is a manifestation of that which we choose with fear in the false self or that which we choose with the bravery of heart in the authentic self.

Once we know our truth, it will always rise within and stir our spirit being to guide our human experiences in the direction of who we were created to be, until our lives become the mirror of our truth. My spirit being was showing up in my human experience, and I felt a fire within my soul that I barely recognized, but I owned it, unapologetically.

My island was devastated, my people were suffering, and I charged forward to unite a people to march for justice. In that whirlwind of events, I found myself facing a different battle. This time, I was battling to shatter the confinements that the external world imposed on me, trying to keep me in my "lane."

What do you do when you discover your authentic self, and in knowing your truth, you realize your power—only to have the world try to stifle you and take it away, because it's not ready for women who are fearless and limitless?

I was on a new journey, a journey that once again took me back to the past; only this time it wasn't just my individual past but my collective past.

It was no surprise that I had to begin with the knowledge and awareness that [his]story was written without [her] story, but how did [his]tory capture her story? And how does the collective story shape my individual story? Could how I see the world and define myself in the world as a woman be different if the story was told by women and their voices had not been silenced throughout [his]tory?

I was on a new quest to see and relearn the world—unapologetically me, embracing all that I am, all woman. But first, I had to learn to dismantle all the false concepts I adopted according to how the world defined me as a woman.

As fate would have it, my name derives from Eve, so I started there, from the beginning. The genesis of when men turned givers of life into a liability of impending demise for human kind. The moment our genetic makeup was marked as inheritably poor in judgment, vulnerable to victimization, and weak, whose only atonement was a whore who saved the men that eventually became the lineage of the savior who could only be birthed by a virgin.

Since the beginning of time, women who have birthed life by boldly, fearlessly, and courageously stepping out and conquering the unknown have been characterized into two groups in [his]story, whores and saints. An evil that could not be corrected in early times because only men were believed to bear the correct genetic makeup to be philosophers and the great influencers in recorded history according to his[story].

Thankfully, there is an ongoing revolution to raise the silenced voices of our heroines in the past and current times, which allows us to see the great plethora of personified divinity in women that have made, and continue to make, great contributions to shaping the world as we know it. I know for a fact, my women tribe, shaped my world. I was captivated, the journey continued. My evolution is my revolution- the end is only the beginning.

The Next Chapter: The Power of The Authentic Self.

About the Author

Before earning degrees at Rutgers University and NYU and devoting her life and a successful career to helping global victims of violent crimes and social injustice, Evelyn was a survivor herself. Despite it all, Evelyn did not allow her past to hold her back. Instead, she let it fuel her tenacious spirit to push through it all and make a difference for women and children who are suffering across the globe.

This book begins by describing Evelyn's past, but continues forward and, with a twist of fate, becomes a real-life breakthrough story that is enriching, empowering, and awe-inspiring.

Evelyn is a native Puerto Rican-New Yorker, but to date, she has travelled across the globe to quench her thirst for truth, knowledge, growth and self-discovery, while honoring her commitment to service. She has personally served, directed and volunteered in countless international initiatives in the public and private sector.

A trailblazer, humanitarian, advocate and thought leader, she is a change agent who fiercely and fearlessly charges forward making an impact in countless lives, while allowing the journey to be the gateway to her authentic self.

With her unique blend of spiritual and social consciousness, her work once again, leads the path to a new school of thought in "The Woman in the Mirror".

CPSIA information can be obtained
at www.ICGtesting.com
Printed in the USA
BVHW071255191118
533502BV00005B/445/P